LEADERS
WITHOUT BORDERS
9 ESSENTIALS FOR EVERYDAY LEADERS

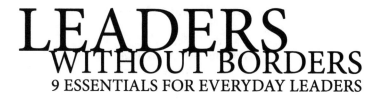

LEADERS
WITHOUT BORDERS
9 ESSENTIALS FOR EVERYDAY LEADERS

DOUG DICKERSON

Leaders Without Borders

Published by
Tremendous Life Books
206 West Allen Street
Mechanicsburg, PA 17055

Copyright © 2010 by Doug Dickerson

ISBN: 978-1-933715-99-5

Book Production Services Provided by Gregory A. Dixon

Printed in the United States of America

DEDICATION

I would like to dedicate this book to my leading ladies—
my wife, Alicia, and my two beautiful daughters, Katelyn
and Kara, who are the loves and joy of my life—and to
my parents, Carolyn Dickerson and my late father, Carl
Dickerson, who from an early age in my life modeled
leadership in the home.

CONTENTS

FOREWORD

L eadership is a challenge. Done right, it takes clear thinking
and hard work. I rarely like easy answers because they're
usually unrealistic. I do, however, like books that challenge
a leader's thinking and provide him or her with new insights
that prompt action. This book by Doug Dickerson is that kind
of book.

A plethora of books are available on how to lead, but a
shortage of books that fully explains why one might desire to
lead in the first place. *Leaders without Borders* includes plenty
of examples and ideas about how to lead, but it goes further
and addresses matters of the heart. In it, you'll find insights
into the why of leadership and not just the how-to. You'll be
challenged in your thinking about what is truly important, and
you'll be asked to contemplate the larger issues of leadership
and life.

As leaders we need to identify the borders that are all around
us and transcend them to reach our maximum potential. Borders
can limit us or leverage us, depending on how we understand
them. Doug Dickerson's book—the definitive guide to how to
recognize and overcome these borders—is filled with real-life
examples and anecdotes that will stay with you as you face
your daily opportunities to excel.

Borderless leadership is passionate leadership. It transcends
the identity of simply what you do and focuses on your higher
purpose, not just an addition to your résumé. Doug shows how
leaders often see the value of leading, or have a desire to lead,
but fail to understand leadership's greater purpose. This book
will help you discover the purpose of leadership.

Borderless leadership requires separation—a separation that

occurs when you embrace your dream and move with passion, when you break from the pack and when you empower your team. Doug also provides tools to help you balance your priorities so that you can stay focused on what is truly important.

Leaders without Borders will ensure that you make a more positive and measurable mark. The privilege of loving, knowing, and respecting those people whom you lead is what leadership is all about. This book will help you discover that what you can learn from them and what they can learn from you is unlimited.

I commend you for investing the time to become a student of leadership. As I say in my work—and I know Doug agrees—leadership doesn't *make* a difference; leadership *is* the difference.

Mark Sanborn
President, Sanborn & Associates Inc.
An idea studio for leadership development

PART ONE

BORDERS WITHIN US—FACING THE CHALLENGE OF PERSONAL LEADERSHIP

CHAPTER ONE

PASSION

Embracing the challenge of personal leadership is the beginning of expanding the sphere of your influence. Whether you are the CEO of your business or serve elsewhere in the organizational structure, one thing is for sure: the boundaries of your leadership are limitless if you are devoted to developing your personal leadership skills.

In order to reach your potential as a leader, you must not only embrace your passion but identify it.

In his book *Halftime: Changing Your Game Plan from Success to Significance*, Bob Buford writes, "Most people never discover their 'one thing.' But part of what is so unsettling about approaching the end of the first half of our lives is that we know it is out there somewhere."

Finding your one thing—your passion as a leader—is life-transforming. As Buford says, "It is discovering what's true about yourself, rather than overlaying someone else's truth on you or injecting someone else's goals onto your personality."

Each person's passions, gifts, and abilities are different, and where those God-given gifts take you is a personal journey. I would like to offer up a few questions to help you in the discovery process of understanding what your passion is.

First, what tugs at your heart? Beneath the exterior shell that others see is something that stirs you. In leadership, what stirs your heart is likely an area in which you are going to be effective. Your passion as a leader is developed by what moves you at your core.

What tugs at your heart gives you direction as a leader. Charles Parkhurst said, "The heart has eyes that the brain knows nothing of." Discovering your passion as a leader is about following a passion that likely already exists. It is a calling to causes greater than self. What is it?

Second, what is your gift? Identifying what tugs at your heart propels you in the right direction. Understanding your gift is to know where you fit in the puzzle. No one person can do it all, but discovering your passion and matching it with your gifts is the way to excel as a leader.

Danish philosopher Søren Kierkegaard said, "The thing is to understand myself, to see what God really wishes me to do . . . to find the idea for which I can live and die." When you discover that passion as a leader your influence will transcend the identity of what you do. At this level your identity as a leader will be defined by the passion of your heart.

Finally, what is your purpose? Discovering your purpose leads to your plan; what are you prepared to do about it?

One of golf's immortal moments came when a Scotsman demonstrated the game to President Ulysses Grant. Carefully placing the ball on the tee, he took a mighty swing. The club hit the turf and scattered dirt all over the president's beard and surrounding vicinity, while the ball placidly waited on the tee. Again the Scotsman swung, and again he missed. President Grant waited patiently through six tries and then quietly stated, "There seems to be a fair amount of exercise in the game, but I fail to see the purpose of the ball."

In leadership, many see the value of leading, or desire to lead, but fail to understand its greater purpose.

What is the one thing you are passionate about as a leader? That is what you have to figure out.

Passion is born out of a dream that resides in your heart.

Taking a dream and turning it into a reality that defines your passion and purpose is to rise to a level of leadership that separates you from the rest of the pack.

Dr. Martin Luther King Jr. embraced his dream with a passion and turned it into reality that defined his legacy.

Aristotle said, "Hope is a waking dream." King's vision was one that awakened a nation and helped to right the course of that nation's history. As was the case in the dream King embraced, your dream will lead you on a path of destiny you must embrace.

Big dreams inspire us to greater causes. On August 28, 1963, tens of thousands descended on the Mall in Washington, D.C., to hear King deliver his famous "I Have a Dream" speech. In it he said, "This note was a promise that all men, yes, black men as well as white men, would be guaranteed the unalienable rights of life, liberty, and the pursuit of happiness."

King was a crusader for equity of rights for all people and races. His dream was for a cause greater than himself in which he was relentless in pursuing. How about you? Is your dream for a cause greater than yourself?

In his book *Rules of Thumb*, Alan M. Webber asks an interesting question: "Would you rather have tepid success with something that doesn't matter or a brilliant failure with something that does?" A big dream sets you on a course of action and for a cause greater than you. The size of your dream determines the sphere of your influence. The greater your influence, the greater the impact you will have.

Big dreams inspire us to greater challenges. In his speech King continued, "As we walk, we must make the pledge that we shall always march ahead. We cannot turn back. . . . I am not unmindful that some of you have come here out of great trials and tribulations. Some of you have come fresh from narrow jail cells. . . . You have been veterans of creative suffering.

Continue to work with the faith that unearned suffering is redemptive."

While tempted to bask in the glory of a dream achieved, remember that dreams are achieved through sacrifice and hard work. Dreams have a tendency to die, not because the dream is unworthy, but because the dreamer gave up too soon.

Anatole France said, "To accomplish great things, we must dream as well as act." King not only had a big dream, but he acted on it and inspired others to join him. Your dream becomes a reality when your heart grows legs and you take the first steps toward achieving it.

Big dreams inspire us with greater courage. King understood the necessity of his dream. He said, "I have a dream that my four little children will one day live in a nation where they will not be judged by the color of their skin but by the content of their character."

On that August day, King didn't just deliver a good speech. He delivered courage and inspiration. He emboldened people to not just dream but to believe that they could be the ones to go forth and make it a reality.

Big dreams have a way of stretching us. John F. Kennedy said, "We need men who can dream of things that never were." Big dreams should not just elevate our imaginations but our hearts to causes greater than ourselves, empower us to face our challenges, and give us the courage to overcome them.

A natural progression begins to unfold in your life as you begin a process of discovering your passion and embracing your dreams. In leadership I have often wondered at what point you separate yourself from others around you, your competition, and your colleagues and move to a higher level. What is the tipping point when a leader parts company with those around him—even when others have equal or greater talents?

In his book *Winning Every Day*, legendary coach Lou Holtz shares a story about taking his Notre Dame football team to the

Sugar Bowl to face the Florida Gators. Notre Dame was the underdog. Could the team pull out a win?

Holtz recalls taking his family to dinner one night before the game and sharing his optimism and how he believed his team could win the game. Holtz said, "I felt like I was on top of the world. While taking our order, the waiter scrutinized me a bit before asking, 'Aren't you Lou Holtz, the Notre Dame coach?' When I told him I was, he said, 'Let me ask you a question. What's the difference between Notre Dame and Cheerios?' I didn't know. He answered, 'Cheerios belong in a bowl, Notre Dame doesn't.'"

Holtz recalls how upset he was over the incident but held to his belief that they could win. Holtz added, "I shrugged off my anger and reminded myself that I knew what our team could do; it didn't matter what anybody else thought. That's the attitude you have to carry into life." In the end, Notre Dame defeated the Gators 39-28.

The *American Heritage Dictionary* defines separation as "the place at which a division or parting occurs." I believe this division or parting in leadership occurs as you identify these four processes.

Separation occurs as you embrace your dream. How many times have you heard someone say, "One of these days I am going to . . ."? What separates you as a leader is when you embrace your dream and dare to act on it.

In his book *Put Your Dream to the Test*, John Maxwell writes, "I don't know what you desire to accomplish or who you will need to include to see your dream come to fruition. You may need only the encouragement and care of one other human being to help you keep going. Or you may need an army. Regardless of your situation, I can tell you that you do need others. The bigger the dream, the greater your need. But here's the good news: the size of your dream determines the size of the people who will be attracted to it."

When you dare to embrace your dream and act on it, you'll never live a day regretting what could have been.

Leadership separation occurs when you excel with passion. Passion is what keeps you up late at night and gets you up early in the morning. Passion is the driving force that transforms you from average to great.

Denis Diderot said, "Only passions, great passions, can elevate the soul to do great things." A leader breaks from the pack when he embraces his dream with a passion unlike anyone else. Passion is one of those rare commodities that resides deeper than head knowledge of a plan and product. Passion resonates from the heart and inspires you to go further.

Leadership separation occurs when you empower your team. When a leader goes to the next level he doesn't go alone. Joe Paterno said, "When a team outgrows individual performance and learns team confidence, excellence becomes a reality." Nothing propels confidence like an empowered team committed to achieving common goals.

Rising to the next level is a team effort. Yogi Berra said, "Every organization needs team players, people you can always depend on." Empowered team members will take you further than you can go by yourself. The more you empower your team, the further you can go.

Leadership separation occurs when you enjoy the journey. I can't imagine anything worse than not enjoying the journey as a leader. I have seen up close the effects of the rat race and how it robs one of enjoying the moment. One's dream, passion, and team efforts means little if you are miserable.

When the late Nadine Stair of Louisville, Kentucky, was eighty-five years old, she was asked what she would do if she had her life to live over again.

Stair replied, "I would make more mistakes next time. I would relax. I would limber up. I would be sillier than I have been this trip. I would take fewer things seriously. I would take more chances. I would climb more mountains and swim more rivers. I would eat more ice cream and less beans. I would perhaps have more actual troubles, but would have fewer imaginary ones."

Stair reminds us to enjoy the journey; after all, getting there is half the fun. A successful leader will take himself and others around him on a journey of new possibilities when he leads from a heart of passion.

CHAPTER TWO

PRIORITIES

One of the challenges of good leadership is maintaining priorities. Many things compete for your time, energy, and money, and learning to say no to many good things can be taxing.

I read a story of a young and successful executive who was traveling down a neighborhood street, going a bit too fast in his new Jaguar. He was watching for kids darting out from between cars and slowed down when he thought he saw something.

No children appeared, but instead a brick smashed into the Jaguar's passenger-side front door. The driver slammed on the brakes and spun the car back to the spot from where the brick had been thrown.

The driver jumped out of the car, grabbed some kid, and pushed him up against the parked car, shouting, "What was that all about and who are you? Just what the heck are you doing?" Building up a head of steam, he continued, "That's a new car, and that brick you threw is going to cost you a lot of money. Why did you do it?"

"Please, mister, please, I'm sorry. I didn't know what else to do!" pleaded the youngster. "I threw the brick because no one else would stop."

Tears were dripping down the boy's chin as he pointed to the parked car. "It's my brother," he said. "He rolled off the curb and fell out of his wheelchair, and I can't lift him up."

Sobbing, the boy asked the executive, "Would you please help me get him back into his wheelchair? He's hurt and he's too heavy for me."

Moved beyond words, the driver tried to swallow the rapidly swelling lump in his throat. He lifted the young man back into the wheelchair and took out his handkerchief and wiped the scrapes and cuts, checking to see that everything was going to be okay.

"Thank you, sir. And God bless you," the grateful child said to him. The man then watched as the little boy pushed his brother to the sidewalk toward their home. It was a long walk back to his Jaguar . . . a long, slow walk. He never did repair the side door. He kept the dent to remind him not to go through life so fast that someone has to throw a brick to get your attention.

Priorities in leadership have to be guarded like your bottom line. When flooded with many good things competing for your time and attention, having a brick thrown your way may not be a bad thing. Here are a few times when it might be useful.

We need a brick when we forget our family. Leaders take on many responsibilities that compete for family time. There is no higher calling for a leader than to be a leader in the home first. Leadership begins at home. If you haven't been successful in the living room, success in the boardroom won't matter.

Frank Sinatra said, "I would like to be remembered as a man who had a wonderful time living life, a man who had good friends, a fine family, and I don't think I could ask for anything more than that, actually." Sinatra had a decent perspective.

We need a brick when we forget our friends. Colleagues who work hard and share your successes need to be remembered. Muhammad Ali said, "Friendship is the hardest thing in the world to explain. It's not something you learn in school. But if you haven't learned the meaning of friendship, you really haven't learned anything."

In your workplace, remember the friends who have helped you achieve and attain the success you now enjoy. When colleagues are befriended it increases morale and keeps you grounded as a leader.

We need a brick when we forget that there are things in life bigger than us. The end game is not in what we get, but in what we give. In other words, it's not about us. The fulfillment of our dreams and aspirations is found in causes greater than us.

Calvin Coolidge said, "No enterprise can exist for itself alone. It ministers to some great need, it performs some great service, not for itself but for others; or failing therein, it ceases to be profitable and ceases to exist." Leaders should be striving not only to lift themselves to a higher level but also to raise the level of awareness of the organization toward serving others.

As Coolidge understood in his day, so too we must understand in ours that properly balanced priorities are essential for staying focused and on course. When a leader is focused on the right priorities, it can make the difference between success and failure.

Don McCullough shares a story of hope and encouragement from his writing, *Walking from the American Dream*, that illustrates this point. McCullough writes, "During World War II, England needed to increase its production of coal. Winston Churchill called together labor leaders to enlist their support. At the end of his presentation he asked them to picture in their minds a parade which he knew would be held in Piccadilly Circus after the war.

"First, he said, would come the sailors who had kept the vital sea lanes open. Then would come the soldiers who had come home from Dunkirk and then gone on to defeat Rommel in Africa. Then would come the pilots who had driven the Luftwaffe from the sky.

"Last of all, he said, would come a long line of sweat-stained, soot-streaked men in miner's caps. Someone would cry from the crowd, 'And where were you during the critical days of our struggle?' And from ten thousand throats would come the answer, 'We were deep in the earth with our faces to the coal.'"

Inspiring others is one of the characteristics of a good leader. Churchill was a man of great motivation and leadership whom I have enjoyed studying over the years. He encouraged a nation during its darkest hours and lifted the hopes and aspirations of his people.

With skill and a steady hand of leadership, Churchill modeled why priorities are essential and how when we incorporate them in our lives, we can become more effective leaders.

He reminded them of the mission. With his words he painted the big picture of why their commitment was crucial in those dark days. He knew the task was difficult. He was aware of the overwhelming obstacles before them. But instead of focusing on the difficulty, he painted a picture to inspire them; it was a picture of victory.

As a leader, your task is not just to picture success in your own mind but to transfer the vision to others. When your team sees what you see, they are inspired to go there with you.

At the dedication ceremony of Disney World in Orlando, Florida, Mrs. Disney was being introduced to speak. Her husband, Walt Disney, had already passed away by this time. During the introductory remarks, the emcee said, "I wish Walt Disney could have seen this." Upon taking the podium, Mrs. Disney said, "He did."

Churchill's reminder was not just of the mission but encouragement to stay the course, to not lose sight of what was most important.

He reminded them of the power of teamwork. In calling upon their services and sacrifices, he pointed out the various workers and their contributions.

He spoke of the sailors, the soldiers, and the pilots who

would be honored in the parade. Then he did something fascinating as a leader. He spoke of the men who were deep in the earth with their faces to the coal.

You see, not every team member is a visible team player, but every team player is valuable. Churchill knew that some would call into question where the scraggly miners were during the conflict. He knew some would call into question their level of commitment and sacrifice. But Churchill knew of their service and would not allow them to be forgotten. That's why when he painted the picture of the parade, they were included.

Without team members with their faces to the coal, you may not enjoy the success you do. Ralph Waldo Emerson said, "Trust men and they will be true to you; treat them greatly and they will show themselves great."

You will experience success in your organization when you focus on your mission and unleash the power of teamwork. And if you want to know who the real heroes on your team are, they are easy to find: they have their faces to the coal.

Leaders with a proper understanding of an organization's goals and objectives not only inspire the organization, but inspire the people with balanced priorities to achieve success.

While maintaining priorities requires discipline, a good leader is also curious when it comes to leadership style. A good leader allows a healthy curiosity to elevate one's leadership skill and consequently that of the organization.

A sign in a window of an English company read, "We have been established for over one hundred years and have been pleasing and displeasing customers ever since. We have made money and lost money, suffered effects of coal nationalization, coal rationing, government control, and bad payers. We have been cussed and discussed, messed about, lied to, held up, and swindled. The only reason we stay in business is to see what happens next."

The late Walter Pater said, "What we have to do is be forever curiously testing new opinions and courting new impressions." I believe that curious leaders are the lifeblood of any organization. I also believe that when leaders cease to be curious, creativity begins to wane.

What are you curious about as a leader? What grabs your attention and captures your imagination?

A curious leader asks a lot of questions. Albert Einstein said, "The important thing is to not stop questioning. Curiosity has its own reason for existing. One cannot help but be in awe when he contemplates the mysteries of eternity, of life, or the marvelous structure of reality." Asking questions is the pathway to understanding.

Remember when your children were small and their eyes were opening to the world around them? When my two girls were growing up, like many parents, I thought I would go crazy with all of the questions of, "Daddy, is the moon made of cheese?" or "Daddy, how does Santa Claus get in the house when we don't have a chimney?" Remember those days?

Perhaps the next gathering around the table in the boardroom ought to be a return to the innocence and wonderment with eyes wide open to new possibilities that you did not realize existed. I think James Thurber was on to something when he said, "It is better to know some of the questions than all of the answers."

A curious leader challenges old assumptions. Your way forward is through fresh eyes and clear thinking. Alan Alda said, "Begin challenging your own assumptions. Your assumptions are your windows on the world. Scrub them off every once in a while, or light won't come in."

A curious leader is in the forefront of this new paradigm of challenge and must make curiosity comfortable for those more skeptical. Guardians of tradition no doubt feel threatened by new ways of thinking, not understanding the greater threat of maintaining the status quo.

Steven R. Covey said, "We simply assume the way we see things is the way they really are or the way they should be. And our attitudes and behaviors grow out of those assumptions." Curiosity is the way out of the rut many organizations find themselves in. The day your team is free to challenge old assumptions is the day your organization begins to rise to a new level."

Curious leaders are willing to take risks. The end result of questions and challenges to old assumptions are but one thing: action. Think of all the modern conveniences of life that you enjoy today. We enjoy them because at some point, questions were asked, assumptions were challenged, and decisions were made.

On September 12, 1962, President John F. Kennedy spoke at Rice University where he delivered his famous speech challenging the nation to reach for the stars and put a man on the moon by the end of the decade.

Kennedy said, "We choose to go to the moon. We choose to go to the moon in this decade and do all the other things, not because they are easy, but because they are hard, because that goal will serve to organize and measure the best of our energies and skills, because that challenge is one that we are willing to accept, one we are unwilling to postpone, and one in which we intend to win, and the others, too."

Was the goal lofty, inspiring, and risky? The obvious answer is yes. Yet Kennedy believed it was attainable. Curious leaders are not satisfied with the status quo and believe the challenges before them are worth the effort of big dreams and risks.

The fundamental characteristic for leaders in establishing priorities is to rightly handle the truth in all their relationships. When a leader is speaking honestly with those around him, trust is established. While it is easy to speak the truth when the news is good, it is equally important to do so when times are tough.

Honesty is an essential ingredient through which leadership flows and how all other relationships within your organization exist. The concept sounds primal, but it's one of which we need to be reminded.

Winston Churchill said, "Men occasionally stumble over the truth, but most of them pick themselves up and hurry off as if nothing ever happened." If your organization is going to thrive, and your leadership is going to be effective, the truth must always win out.

Leaders must speak the truth. Mark Twain said, "Truth is more of a stranger than fiction." Whether it is casting vision for the future of the organization or evaluating the performance of a team member, leaders must speak the truth.

Leaders also must hear the truth. Burton Bigelow said, "Very few big executives want to be surrounded by 'yes' men. Their greatest weakness is the fact that 'yes' men build up around the executive a wall of fiction, when what the executive wants most of all is plain facts." A wise leader does not want to be shielded from the truth, but exposed to it.

Speaking the truth to the leader must be done constructively and with respect. John Maxwell said, "If you've never spoken up to your leaders and told them what they need to hear, then it will take courage. But if you are willing to speak up, you can help your leader and yourself." Examine the motives when speaking to your leader. Be sure that you are not just promoting your own agenda but the best interest of the team.

Leaders must act on the truth. Decisions that leaders make today have consequences for the organization tomorrow. A sharp leader has the intuition to see what is going on around him and is surrounded by honest advisors to help chart the course.

The major lesson as it pertains to priorities is to understand and value the most important things, and not to get confused about our priorities. Architect Frank Lloyd Wright once told of an incident that may have seemed insignificant at the time, but had a profound influence on the rest of his life. The winter when he was nine years old, he was walking across a snow-covered field with his reserved, no-nonsense uncle.

As the two of them reached the far end of the field, his uncle stopped him. He pointed out his own tracks in the snow, straight and true as an arrow's flight, and then young Frank's tracks meandering all over the field. "Notice how your tracks wander aimlessly from the fence to the cattle to all the woods and back again," his uncle said. "And see how my tracks aim directly to my goal. There is an important lesson in that."

Years later the world-famous architect liked to tell how this experience had greatly contributed to his philosophy in life. "I determined right then," he would say with a twinkle in his eyes, "not to miss most things in life, as my uncle had."

It is easy to get so caught up in the grind of life that encompasses all of us as leaders that our tracks do not wander perhaps quite as much as they ought. Yes, we should keep our focus and reach goals, and see dreams come true, but allowing our tracks to wander a bit makes the journey more enjoyable.

Imagine the tracks that you have left thus far on your journey. Are your tracks like that of the uncle, a straight set of tracks that led you toward a desired goal? Or perhaps they resemble those of Frank, who took the scenic route to the same destination?

When arriving at their desired destination, I can only imagine the stories Frank could have shared with his uncle as he strolled by the fence to observe the cattle or of something spotted by the edge of the woods. Through the eyes of the young architect or through your eyes as a leader leaving tracks, the possibilities are endless.

A first-grader wondered why her father brought home a briefcase full of work every evening. Her mother explained, "Daddy has so much to do that he can't finish it all at the office."

"Well, then," asked the child innocently, "why don't they put him in a slower group?" The father may not necessarily need to be in a slower group but, like many leaders, needs to start making a different set of tracks.

Wright said he adopted his philosophy not to miss the most important things in life based on that experience with his uncle. As you set out to make tracks as a leader, here are some ideas on moving forward.

Don't miss the simple lessons. Many are looking for the next big experience that will satisfy or make them happy. I've found, especially living along the Atlantic coast, that a sunrise or sunset walk along the beach is one of the most spectacular things I can enjoy.

Elbert Hubbard made reference to the fact that life often consists of one challenge after another. This is why enjoying the simplicity of it is so rewarding. Nothing is more humbling than a walk along the beach to serve as a reminder that if God can keep the oceans in check, he can then also make order out of my life.

Don't miss the simple joys. Misunderstanding the source of joy is what causes most to miss it. Sister Mary Rose McGeady said, "There is no greater joy nor greater reward than to make a fundamental difference in someone's life." Simple joys are found in what we do for others as we make our tracks. When you as a leader remember to spread joy, it will make someone else's load lighter.

Don't miss the simple paths. John Hope Franklin said, "We must get beyond textbooks, go out into the bypaths . . . and tell the world the glories of our journey." The simple paths may not lead you where you expected, but that is the beauty of them. The simple paths become spectacular when you realize they are not accidental but destined.

Leaders must pay attention to priorities. Personal success is the springboard to organizational success. Dwight Eisenhower said, "The older I get, the more wisdom I find in the ancient rule of taking first things first—a process which often reduces the most complex human problem to a manageable proportion." When priorities are established in a leader's private life it sets the agenda for corporate priorities.

Defining your personal priorities begins as you map out the issues of faith, family, business, and finance. A sage leader learns to delegate his or her time wisely and finds a sense of balance in life. At the end of the day, heed the advice of Charles Mays, who said, "Make sure the thing you're living for is worth dying for."

CHAPTER THREE

OPTIMISM

Over the years I have been privileged to travel to many parts of the world and experience some truly amazing cultures. From the islands of the Caribbean and Central and South America, to London, Athens, and Jerusalem, each stop on the journey has been rewarding. Yet for all of those experiences, living along coastal South Carolina is still quite a treat.

Rich in history, wonderful beaches, and some of the best cuisine you will find anywhere in the world, the South Carolina coast is truly an amazing place to live. One of the annual traditions here is the Family Circle Cup women's tennis tournament on Daniel Island. The world's top stars compete annually at this world-class facility for the coveted title. Past champions of the Family Circle Cup include Chris Evert, Steffi Graf, Gabriela Sabatini, Martina Hingis, Venus Williams, and her sister Serena, to name a few.

The tennis world was recently shocked and saddened by the news that Martina Navratilova had developed a noninvasive form of breast cancer. Her prognosis is good, and all wish her the very best in her recovery.

Navratilova's tennis career is a benchmark for aspiring tennis stars. She won Wimbledon eight times, won every Grand Slam at least two times each, and in 1984 held all Grand Slam titles simultaneously. Her accomplishments on and off the court have earned her the respect of fans worldwide.

As leaders we are not immune from disappointments and

setbacks. "Trials, temptations, disappointments," said James Buckham. "All these are helps instead of hindrances, if one uses them rightly. They not only test the fiber of our character but strengthen it. Every conquering temptation represents a new fund of moral energy. Every trial endured and weathered in the right spirit makes a soul nobler and stronger than it was before." Simply put, what happens to us is not as important as how we respond to it.

The choices you make as a leader today set the course for where you go as a leader tomorrow. Three factors are worthy of consideration.

1. *The factor of a positive response.* You are in command of your response. Henry Van Dyke said, "There is no personal charm so great as the charm of a cheerful temperament." As a leader, you set the tone not only for yourself but for your organization by the way you react to the things that happen to you.

A positive response is not a willful denial of the reality that exists. Your response, however, reflects the realization that whatever happened is only a snapshot of one moment in the larger picture of your destiny. When you choose not to be defined by one negative moment, but rather redefine it for good, you have chosen a positive response.

2. *The factor of a positive attitude.* I like Herm Albright's lighthearted observation: "A positive attitude may not solve all of your problems, but it will annoy enough people to make it worth the effort." A positive attitude in the midst of negative circumstances is exactly the right prescription to turn things around.

While no one can deny that Thomas Edison was a man of accomplishment, he also suffered great setbacks. Yet Edison said, "I never did a day's work in all my life. It was all fun." What a great attitude. The right attitude propelled him to unimaginable accomplishment, and it can do the same for you.

3. *The factor of positive perseverance.* When you choose a positive response to negative circumstances, you begin to experience exponential growth as a leader. Your reactions— positive or negative—set in motion the laws of reciprocity. The choices you make have a great impact.

Emerson said, "That which we persist in doing becomes easier, not that the task itself has become easier, but that our ability to perform it has become easier." Your reaction as a leader is charting a course for your future, so choose it wisely.

Champions like Martina Navratilova may have been stunned by a doctor's report, and you may be reeling from the effects of the economy, but if your choice moving forward is a positive one, you are already one step ahead of the game.

Consider the story told of Thomas Jefferson during his days as president. He and a group of companions were traveling across country on horseback. They came to a river that had left its banks because of a recent downpour. The swollen river had washed the bridge away.

Each rider was forced to ford the river on horseback, fighting for his life against the rapid currents. The very real possibility of death threatened each rider, causing a traveler who was not part of their group to step aside and watch.

After several had plunged in and made it to the other side, the stranger asked President Jefferson if he would ferry him across the river. The president agreed without hesitation. The man climbed on, and shortly thereafter the two of them made it safely to the other side.

As the stranger slid off the back of the saddle onto the ground, one in the group asked him, "Tell me, why did you select the president to ask this favor of?"

The man was shocked, admitting he had no idea it was the president who had helped him. "All I know," he said, "is that on some of your faces was written the answer 'no,' and on some of them was the answer 'yes.' His was a 'yes' face."

When it comes to the climate in your organization, what does your face say about you? Are you an optimist or a pessimist? Sure, times are challenging, but the face you wear is giving signals to your team. A strong leader is one who does not shy away from reality, but looks through the lens of optimism in the face of challenges.

An optimistic leader confronts his fears. The men riding with Jefferson had to confront a raging river and risk death to cross to the other side. One by one they took the plunge and made their way across.

I am not recommending reckless abandon in your business dealings. I would, however, suggest that you not allow fear to paralyze you to the point that you are afraid to take risks. Legendary football coach Vince Lombardi said, "We would accomplish many more things if we did not think of them as impossible." Obstacles along your path may not be of your choosing or creation, but the way in which you confront them is.

An optimistic leader gives others confidence. The stranger at the river chose Jefferson, not because the stranger knew Jefferson was the president, but because Jefferson exuded a confidence that the man saw and in which he took comfort. As a leader, the confidence that you exude gives cues to your team's members.

Rudy Giuliani said, "Leaders need to be optimists. Their vision is beyond the present." If as a leader you are weighed down by fear and doubt and are not looking to the future, your team will suffer. Jefferson's face instilled all the confidence one man needed to face his fear. What does your face say about you?

An optimistic leader looks for the good in all situations. The story is told of two boys who were twins—one an incurable optimist, one a pessimist. The parents were worried about the extremes of behavior and attitude and finally took the boys to a psychologist. The psychologist observed them for a while and said they could easily be helped.

He said that they had a room filled with all the toys a boy could want. They would put the pessimist in that room and allow him to enjoy life. They also had another room that they filled with horse manure. They put the optimist in that room. They observed both boys through one-way mirrors. The pessimist continued to be a pessimist, stating that he had no one to play with.

They went to look at the optimist, and were astounded to find him digging through the manure. The psychologist ran into the room and asked what on earth the boy was doing. He replied that with all the manure, he was sure there had to be a pony in the room somewhere.

Sometimes you have to dig through some unpleasant things to find the good, but all things worthwhile require effort. Regardless of how difficult things may appear around you, carry the face that says yes.

An optimistic leader will certainly have moments of being tested. Not everything will go according to script, so an optimistic leader must also learn to be flexible.

Apollo 13 is one of my favorite movies. It chronicles the Apollo 13 space mission that was to carry three astronauts to the moon. Instead of landing on the moon, the mission was scrubbed due to an explosion onboard the spacecraft.

One famous line in the movie occurs right after the explosion when Tom Hanks, who portrayed astronaut Jim Lovell, says, "Houston, we have a problem." The other memorable line comes from Ed Harris, who plays the role of NASA flight director Gene Kranz. After overhearing some negative speculation on the chances of returning the astronauts safely, Kranz says, "With all due respect, sir, I believe this is gonna be our finest hour."

How does the same set of negative circumstances make a

disaster for one person and success for another? What makes the difference between disaster for one and the finest hour for another? There are a few things worth remembering when it comes to leadership, especially in times of crisis and maintaining a high level of optimism.

Leaders must remember that not everything goes according to script. Years of hard work and preparation went into the launch of Apollo 13, and the defect that caused the explosion was in place before the Apollo crew was even named.

Thomas Edison said, "If I find ten thousand ways something won't work, I haven't failed. I am not discouraged, because every wrong attempt discarded is another step forward." How you react when things blow up determines for you a positive outcome or a negative one.

Leaders must remember that success is discovered in adversity. Not every bump in the road is necessarily a bad thing. We can get so accustomed to smooth sailing that when challenges come, we don't know how to react. In *Apollo 13*, Ed Harris made the point that an American had never been lost in space and he was determined not to lose one on his watch! "Failure is not an option," he said.

Horace said, "Adversity has the effect of eliciting talents, which in prosperous circumstances would have lain dormant." Your ability to succeed in the face of adversity will not be far-fetched when you embrace what comes your way with a determination to overcome. It's not that you are sitting around waiting on something to go wrong, but when it does, failure will not be an option for you.

Leaders know that great minds work together. When faced with the challenge of bringing the crew home alive given near-impossible conditions, the NASA crew rose to the occasion and did the impossible.

Creativity in your organization should be encouraged and promoted. In his book *Rules of Thumb*, Alan M. Webber writes,

"Most companies have people who are nothing but idea people and others are implementers. You need them both. Great idea people are rare—and also frequently hard to live with. They see things the rest of us can't see, which is their gift. They can't see what you and I see easily, which is their burden. Still, you need them and they need a home where they can contribute. Your job is to build a bridge the great ideas can walk across, from those who have them to those who make them real."

It's been said that great minds think alike. But if that is the case in your organization, be concerned. If everyone is thinking alike, someone isn't thinking enough. Good leaders pull together the resources of the best and brightest in the organization and build the bridges necessary for overwhelming success.

The next time things go haywire around you, just remember that you are not alone. When times are tough and adversity strikes, let your confident words be, "I believe this is gonna be our finest hour."

Optimism takes on many forms for a leader, beginning as an inward impression that only the leader can cultivate. It matures in the face of difficulty and inspires others to come up to your level to believe that anything is possible.

Life, the saying goes, is a continuous process of getting used to things we hadn't expected. There is no denying that we are living in challenging times. An optimistic leader adjusts in practical ways to life's events and in doing so serves as an agent of optimism.

Harry Truman said, "Men who live in the past remind me of a toy I am sure all of you have seen. The toy is a small wooden bird called the 'Floogie Bird.' Around the Floogie Bird's neck is a reading, "I fly backwards, I don't care where I am going. I just want to see where I've been.'" Flying backward is just not an option for the optimistic leader.

The noted English architect Sir Christopher Wren was supervising the construction of a magnificent cathedral in London. A journalist thought it would be interesting to interview some of the workers, so he chose three and asked them this question, "What are you doing?"

The first replied, "I'm cutting stone for ten shillings a day." The next answered, "I'm putting in ten hours a day on this job." But the third said, "I'm helping Sir Christopher Wren construct one of London's greatest cathedrals."

Optimism is an attitude that leaders choose even when the work seems monotonous or difficult. T. E. Lawrence said, "All men dream but not equally. Those who dream by night in the dusty recesses of their minds awake to find it was all vanity. But the dreamers of the day are dangerous men, for the many act out their dreams with open eyes to make it possible."

You may not have chosen the challenges you face today, and while you may be hard-pressed to find anything good in the difficulty of today, I do believe that tragedy and hardship are never wasted, and an optimistic heart and mind will see you through.

While it may seem impossible, some of the most optimistic leaders are those who have in fact overcome great adversity. Through their perseverance they emerge as the visionaries that organizations want working for them.

I am reminded of the story in ancient times when a king placed a boulder on a roadway. Then he hid and watched to see if anyone would remove the huge rock. Some of the king's wealthiest merchants and couriers came by and simply walked around it. Many blamed the king for not keeping the roads clear, but none did anything about getting the boulder out of the way.

Then a peasant came along carrying a load of vegetables. On approaching the boulder, the peasant laid down his burden and tried to move the stone to the side of the road. After pushing and straining, he finally succeeded. As the peasant picked up his load of vegetables, he noticed a purse lying in the road where the boulder had been. The purse contained many gold coins and a note from the king indicating that the gold was for the person who removed the boulder from the roadway. The peasant learned what many never understand. Every obstacle presents an opportunity to improve one's condition.

Optimistic leaders move boulders. While many avoided the boulder in the road, the peasant faced the challenge head on. Success comes to those who in the face of obstacles work hard to remove them. While some may prefer to sidestep issues, optimistic leaders confront them.

Someone once said, "If Columbus had turned back, no one could have blamed him, but no one would have remembered him." The optimistic person rolls up his sleeves and moves the boulders on his path. While certainly not an easy task, the job will be worth it when it's complete.

Optimistic leaders see the opportunities boulders bring. As a student, fashion designer Sandra Garrett was given a project to design clothing that would go against her natural inclinations—clothes she did not like.

She came up with a line of economical, one-size-fits-all, modular clothing for women. Garrett moved on to a series of jobs in the fashion industry, but she kept thinking about those clothes she'd designed. They intrigued her enough that she eventually began producing them for a boutique in Dallas.

Several businesspeople saw promise in Garrett's clothes, and in 1986 they invested the money to help her start a nationwide chain of shops. The investment paid off. Within a few years, more than $100 million of Garrett's clothes had been sold, and she had made millions in royalties . . . all because she put her natural inclinations aside and investigated something different.

Optimistic leaders embrace the challenges that boulders present and turn them into opportunities from which others walk away. How you view the boulders before you determines the success you will have. For the peasant the boulder was his reward. For Sandra Garrett the reward came in the form of designing clothes that she didn't like at the start.

The truth is, opportunities often come disguised. Not every boulder on your path is an obstacle; it's simply a reward waiting to be discovered.

In his poem "The Road Not Taken," Robert Frost writes, "I shall be telling this with a sigh, somewhere ages and ages hence: Two roads diverged in a wood, and I—I took the one less traveled by, and that has made all the difference." You are on the path you are on for a purpose. So before you curse the boulder on your path or the one who put it there, keep in mind that what lies underneath it could quite possibly change your life.

Optimism does not prevent difficulties or make you immune from them. Optimism, however, empowers you to face difficulties with a confidence that gives you an advantage to overcome them. Robert L. Stevenson said, "You cannot run away from weakness; you must sometime fight it out or perish; and if that be so, why not now, and where you stand?" Now is the time to rise up with courage and be the optimistic leader you were destined to be.

PART TWO

BORDERS AROUND US— THE BLESSING OF OUR LEADERSHIP

CHAPTER FOUR

TEAMWORK

An inspiring story is told about Jimmy Durante on a tour during World War II. Durante, one of the great American entertainers of the twentieth century, was asked to be part of a show for World War II veterans.

He told the organizers that his schedule was very busy and he could only afford a few minutes, but if they wouldn't mind his doing one short monologue and immediately leaving for his next appointment, he would come.

Of course, the show's director agreed happily. But when Jimmy got on stage, something interesting happened. He went through the short monologue and then stayed. The applause grew louder and he kept staying. Pretty soon, he had been on fifteen minutes, twenty, then thirty minutes. Finally, he took a last bow and left the stage. Backstage, someone stopped him and said, "I thought you had to go after a few minutes. What happened?"

Jimmy answered, "I did have to go, but I can show you the reason I stayed. You can see for yourself if you'll look down on the front row." In the front row were two men, each of whom had lost an arm in the war. One had lost his right arm and the other had lost his left. Together, they were able to clap, and that's exactly what they were doing, loudly and cheerfully.

Teamwork is essential in leadership. Possessing the right leadership ingredients on a personal level is multiplied when you take the next step and apply those principles to team leadership. When team members come together in a spirit of cooperation and unified purpose, its chances of success are multiplied.

Babe Ruth said, "The way the team plays as a whole determines its success. You may have the greatest bunch of individual stars in the world, but if they don't play together, the club won't be worth a dime."

How well you work together as a team makes all the difference. What team characteristics are needed for success? How do you turn personal leadership qualities into successful teamwork strategies? Let's examine a few possibilities.

A team player has the right temperament. A team player has a pleasant combination of what the dictionary defines as "the combination of mental, physical and emotional traits of a person; natural disposition."

In other words, team members blend well with others. The team member is not concerned about wanting or needing his own way. The team member thinks in terms of what is best for the whole team, not just his own needs or wants.

A team player sets the right example. A team player models behavior that others aspire to. Mark Twain said, "Few things are harder to put up with than the annoyance of a good example." A strong team player inspires others by a good example of selfless behavior.

A team player has the right attitude. The attitude at the top of the organization sets the tone for the rest of the organization. John Maxwell said, "A leader's attitude is caught by his or her followers more quickly than his or her actions." A team player contributes to the team with a good attitude.

A team player has the right motivation. A strong team player is motivated to perform at his very best. A team player is always thinking of ways to improve and move the team toward success, which requires a willingness to set aside personal agendas for the sake of the team's agenda.

The development of personal leadership is the first step toward successful teamwork. The concept of teamwork in leadership is not about being a chameleon leader, but rather about allowing the best and brightest to collectively bring their unique giftedness together to accomplish what couldn't be done individually.

One thing I have discovered over the years in leadership is that leadership lessons can be found all around us if we are paying attention. Yogi Berra said, "You can learn a lot by watching." In the winter months where I live, it is not uncommon to see geese flying across the evening sky. In *Are You a Goose*, Tom Worsham shares a fascinating story about geese that reflects strong leadership principles of teamwork.

He writes, "When you see geese heading south for the winter flying along in a 'V' formation, you might be interested in knowing that science has discovered why they fly that way. Research has revealed that as each bird flaps his wings, it creates an uplift for the bird immediately behind it. By flying in a 'V' formation, the whole flock adds at least 71 percent greater flying range than if each bird flew on its own.

"Whenever a goose falls out of formation, it suddenly feels the drag of resistance of trying to go it alone. It quickly gets back into formation to take advantage of the lifting power of the bird immediately in front. When the lead goose gets tired, he rotates back in the 'V' and another goose flies to the point.

"The geese honk from behind to encourage those up front to keep up their speed. And finally, when a goose gets sick, or wounded by gunfire and falls out, two other geese fall out of formation and follow it down and protect it. They stay with the goose until it is either able to fly again or dead, and then they launch out on their own or with another formation to catch up with their group. Whoever was the first to call another person a 'silly goose' didn't know enough about geese."

This fascinating story is full of pointed reminders of the

power of teamwork. When learned and applied, it can make a significant difference in the productivity of your organization.

Geese teach us that we can accomplish more when we work together as a team. Individual talent brought you to the team; combining those talents creates a potent force.

Greg Werner observed, "The life of a high achiever is one of give and receive. We receive that which we are first willing to give out. Therefore, to grow and achieve we must first be willing to help others grow and achieve, and, in doing so, the light of reciprocal achievement will brightly shine upon us."

People who share a common vision, mission, or purpose attain that goal more efficiently when they come together as a team. Just as the geese generate thrust as they travel together, your team's thrust causes you to accomplish more when you stick together.

Geese teach us the power of unity. Solidarity of mission and purpose gives strength to organizational goals and make attaining them more realistic. An African proverb says, "When spider webs unite they can tie up a lion."

Unity in the workplace is defined not just by the slaps on the back in times of success but in lifting up teammates when they are down. A unified team wants everyone to succeed.

Geese teach us to share the load. Each team member possesses the necessary skills and talents for the team to be a success. On any given project you may be the point person to bring the team to victory. On another project someone else may have the right skill set to fulfill the mission.

John Maxwell states, "People come together as teams, peers work together, and they make progress because they want the best idea to win." The formula for success is the same across the board; the team succeeds when we let the best ideas win out.

Don't allow insecurity to cripple the productivity of your organization. Set office politics aside, and rally around the best idea and the best team member for the project. A strong leader gladly shares the lead on projects and is a model team player. When the team shares the load, its work is more productive and the rewards are much greater.

A strong leader understands that when it comes to effective teamwork strategies, the team must be able to navigate many potential obstacles that would seek to derail it. Leaders know that cohesion is essential to success. A wise leader does not take an autopilot approach, allowing things to sail along and being detached from the pulse of the organization.

Neither does a sage leader act as a hovering micromanager, smothering any hopes of creativity and community. A smart leader is engaged and is simply a facilitator of a productive environment of people with a shared mission. But sometimes interruptions and distractions occur. How do you handle them?

Casablanca is considered by many as one of the greatest movies of all time. World War II has engulfed Europe, reaching all the way to Rick Blaine's Café American in French-held Morocco. The Nazis have overrun France and are heading into the unoccupied regions of Africa—and all kinds of people are trying to escape them by way of Casablanca.

Blaine's haven is disrupted when his onetime love Ilsa, played by Ingrid Bergman, arrives in the company of a world-renowned resistance leader Victor Laszlo, whose influence the Nazis would very much like to neutralize. She is looking for safe passage, first from Rick, who believes she jilted him for Laszlo, and then from Signor Ferrari, the owner of the rival Blue Parrott.

Casablanca was a big-budget film for its day and was shot almost entirely on sound stages and the studio lot. Based on the play *Everybody Comes to Rick's*, the screenwriters essentially made up the story as they went along, and no one knew exactly how it would end, which may have added to the film's suspense and freshness.

As a bit of trivia, nobody in the film says the line, "Play it again, Sam." Rick and Ilsa both ask Wilson to play the song, but never use those precise words.

In leadership, unexpected interruptions can throw the team off if not properly prepared. Life can be smooth and pleasant one moment, and the next hour, in walks Ilsa. Interruptions can't always be prevented or predicted, but they can be successfully managed. Learning how to recognize them and respond to them will prepare your team for success.

Interruptions come to us in various forms. They appear as unexpected projects with unrealistic deadlines, and likely come underfunded. An interruption might manifest as a key team member who calls in sick, or an unexpected meeting. Sometimes an Ilsa walks in without an appointment and turns things completely upside down.

Whatever your interruption may be, you should be flexible enough to adjust to the situation. If you can't bend, you'll break. What some may see as an interruption to progress may be nothing more than an opportunity in the making.

Thomas Edison said, "Opportunity is missed by most people because it is dressed in overalls and looks like work." Ilsa may look like an interruption in the beginning, but can turn out to be something entirely different in the end.

Interruptions can bring your team together. One of my favorite quotes from *Casablanca* is by Capt. Louis Renault: "Round up the usual suspects." I think the quote typifies the leader who is looking to rally his team. In other words, round up the go-to players who are committed to the vision and purposes of the organization and work together for its success.

Interruptions can be a blessing in disguise. As Rick Blaine says, "Louis, I think this is the beginning of a beautiful friendship." Unexpected interruptions may annoy us, but if we are observant, they can turn out to be something good we never anticipated.

One of my favorite inspirational stories is that of Thomas Edison. His lab was destroyed by a fire on a cold December evening in 1914. At the height of the fire, Edison's son, Charles, frantically searched for his father among the smoke and debris.

He finally found him, calmly watching the scene, his face glowing in the reflection, his white hair blowing in the wind. The next morning Edison looked at the ruins and said, "There is great value in disaster. All our mistakes are burned up. Thank God we can start anew." Three weeks after the fire, Edison managed to deliver his first phonograph.

Quite possibly, unexpected interruptions can be the beginning of something grand that we never expected. And yes, at times, they can be a nuisance. The difference is in keeping the right attitude when they come your way.

Ultimately, teamwork is the mind-set of confident leadership. The fabric of teamwork is a belief that achieving the organization's goals and objectives is accomplished in a sensible, trustworthy fashion.

The challenge for leadership in facilitating teamwork comes not in an overabundance of rules and guidelines but rather by simplifying them. Bureaucracy is not the answer to successful teamwork; it is the obstacle.

The story is told of a man flying in a hot air balloon who realizes he is lost. He reduces height and spots a man down below. He lowers the balloon and shouts, "Excuse me, can you tell me where I am?"

The man below says, "Yes, you are in a hot air balloon, hovering about thirty feet above this field."

"You must work in information technology," says the balloonist.

"I do," replies the man. "How did you know?"

"Well," says the balloonist, "everything you have told me is technically correct, but it is of no use to anyone."

The man below says, "You must work in management."

"I do," replies the balloonist, "but how did you know?"

"Well," says the man, "you don't know where you are or where you are going, but you expect me to be able to help you. You are in the same position you were before we met, but now it's my fault."

Ever had one of those encounters? At some point we all have. Our perceptions often fuel our expectations. Perceptions can be deceptive, and while expectations need to be high, they must also be realistic.

Sharing practical wisdom about the roles of leadership, Alan M. Webber says, "The problem today is too much information sharing and not enough sense making: too many messages, and too many meetings, too many e-mails, too many change programs, too many changes in direction. The problem only gets worse when the stakes go up—when a company is facing a crisis, when it's up against an innovative competitor and the old ways won't work. That's when too many leaders give in to the temptation to ramp up the volume and amp up the adrenaline. The result: an already overtaxed system collapses from overload."

I neither want to overestimate nor underestimate the idea here, but a fresh look at simplicity is in order. The survival of effective teamwork depends on the understanding and execution of simplicity. Here are some considerations to keep in mind.

Simplify your mission. Simplicity of mission is not dumbing down the mission, nor does it equate to less work. It means working with a smarter understanding of the mission and the most efficient ways to achieve its stated purpose.

Simplifying the mission is about people in your organizational structure being able to connect the dots because leadership made sure they saw the big picture and knew where the ship was headed.

To this end, meetings should be intentional and with a purpose. People should be empowered and trusted, and common sense should prevail.

Simplify communication. Survey most people within many organizations today, and one of the top frustrations you'll find is that of communication—or the lack thereof.

Over the years, I have seen up close at times how morale is sacrificed at the expense of clear, open, and relevant communication. When key personnel are kept in the dark, when office politics stifles and hinders progress, the consequences can be costly. Peter Drucker said, "The most important thing in communication is to hear what isn't being said."

Teamwork is enhanced when communication is clear. Consequently, communication must be simple, concise, and clear. Communication is the life blood of your organization. If you don't communicate well internally, don't expect communication to go well externally. Communication has a profound effect on teamwork.

Is your organization about to buckle under from the weight of too much information and not enough sense making? Effective leaders understand that teamwork rises and falls on the power of simplicity in communication.

The power of teamwork is a process of applauding the gifts and talents that each team member brings to the process: by embracing the challenges that confront teamwork as opportunities, by creating a caring environment, and by simplifying communication.

Teamwork is not meant to be a burden, but a blessing. It need not be a fight for survival by voting members off, but a celebration of diversity that makes you stronger. Teamwork is the gateway to your success. Celebrate it.

CHAPTER FIVE

ATTITUDE

In developing leadership around us, attitude is one of those make-or-break characteristics that you must work to your advantage. While all leaders have a certain attitude, only the best have a positive one.

In *A Cup of Chicken Soup for the Soul*, John Kanary shares a story about Charlie Boswell. Charlie was blinded during World War II while rescuing his friend from a tank that was under fire. He was a great athlete before his accident, and in a testimony to his talent and determination, he decided to try a brand-new sport, a sport he never imagined with his eyesight: golf.

Through determination and a deep love for the game he became the National Blind Golf Champion. He won that honor thirteen times. One of his heroes was the great golfer Ben Hogan, so it was truly an honor for Charlie to win the Ben Hogan Award in 1958.

Upon meeting Ben Hogan, Charlie was awestruck and stated that he had one wish: to play one round of golf with the great Ben Hogan. Hogan agreed that playing a round of golf together would be an honor for him as well, as he had heard about all of Charlie's accomplishments and truly admired his skills.

"Would you like to play for money, Mr. Hogan?" blurted out Charlie.

"I can't play you for money, it wouldn't be fair," said Hogan.

"Aw, come on, Mr. Hogan . . . a thousand dollars per hole!"

"I can't. What would people think of me, taking advantage of you and your circumstances?" replied the sighted golfer.

"Chicken, Mr. Hogan?"

"Okay," blurted out a frustrated Hogan, "but I am going to play my best."

"I wouldn't expect anything else," said a confident Boswell.

"You're on, Mr. Boswell. You name the time and place."

A very self-assured Boswell responded, "10 o'clock . . . tonight!"

That humorous story reminds us that having the right attitude can level the playing field for you not just on a personal level but professionally as well. Leadership expert John Maxwell said, "A leader's attitude is caught by his followers more quickly than his or her actions." While we can't always control what happens to us, we are in control of our attitude. The choice we make determines our future.

We level the playing field when we refuse to allow circumstances to defeat us. In tough economic times, it's a struggle for many. But when we face the challenges of uncertain times with the right attitude, we level the playing field.

C. S. Lewis said, "Every time you make a choice you are turning the control part of you, the part that chooses, into something a little different from what it was before. And taking your life as a whole, with all your innumerable choices, you are slowly turning this control thing either into a heavenly creature or a hellish one." You level the playing field with wise choices and right attitudes.

We level the playing field by setting the right example. As a leader your attitude should be the thermostat your team is set at. Simply put, your action as a leader multiplies the reaction of the team. When the leader's attitude is strong, then the team's attitude is strong. What type of example are you setting?

We level the playing field with high expectations. High

expectations create an environment that is ripe for success. Attitude is the lens through which you look at your world. It's how you look at yourself as a leader, how you see others, and how your team embraces its mission and purpose.

The story of the hummingbird is a classic example of the choices we make with regard to our attitude. Both the hummingbird and the vulture fly over our nation's deserts. All vultures see is rotting meat, because that is what they look for. They thrive on that diet.

But the hummingbirds ignore the smelly flesh of dead animals. Instead they look for the colorful blossoms of desert plants. The vultures live on what was. They live on the past. They fill themselves with what is dead and gone.

But hummingbirds live on what is. They seek new life. They fill themselves with freshness and life. Each bird finds what it is looking for. We all do.

In *The Fred Factor,* my friend Mark Sanborn writes, "Freds know that one of the most exciting things about life is that we awake each day with the ability to reinvent ourselves. No matter what happened yesterday, today is a new day. While we can't deny the struggles and setbacks, neither should we be restrained by them."

Don't let the circumstances that life brings your way restrain you. Embrace them and be emboldened by them. Yes, you will face struggles and disappointments, but the choice you make with regard to your attitude will make all the difference.

In his book *The Pitfalls of Positive Thinking*, Donald McCullough shares interesting insights from individuals considered persons of accomplishment, yet who struggled with personal disappointments.

McCullough writes, "Alexander the Great conquered Persia, but broke down and wept because his troops were too exhausted to push on to India. John Quincy Adams, the sixth president of the United States—not a Lincoln, perhaps, but a decent leader—wrote in his diary: 'My life has been spent in vain and idle aspirations, and in ceaseless rejected prayers that something would be the result of my existence beneficial to my species.'"

Robert Louis Stevenson wrote words that continue to delight and enrich our lives, yet what did he write for his epitaph? "Here lies one who meant well, and tried a little, and failed much." Cecil Rhodes opened up Africa and established an empire, but what were his dying words? "So little done, so much to do."

Let's be honest: we all have had our share of disappointments and setbacks. On a professional level, how you deal with disappointments sets the tone for the organization. In *Life 101,* Peter McWilliams writes, "The simple solution for disappointment depression: Get up and get moving. Physically move. Do. Act. Get going." How you handle disappointments determines your destination.

Personal disappointment is one of the hardest situations from which to recover. Usually disappointment comes because of something we did. Perhaps our disappointment came from a poor decision, or how we responded to something that was out of our control.

When it comes to personal disappointments, forgive yourself; cut yourself some slack, and get moving. Once you have identified the cause of your personal disappointment you are now empowered to make corrections. Identify what went wrong, accept responsibility, and move on. Simply put, life is too short to wallow in self-pity.

In *Failing Forward,* John Maxwell says, "Someone who is unable to get over previous hurts and failures is held hostage by the past. The baggage he carries around makes it very difficult for him to move forward. In fact, in more than thirty years of working with people, I have yet to meet a successful person who continuously dwelled on his past difficulties."

Life is filled with disappointments and mistakes, but we must not allow them to own us. In his book *Attitudes That Attract Success*, Wayne Cordeiro writes, "Each of us will be surrounded with problems at times, and will often find ourselves steeped in hot water. But remember that the event will soon pass. The event is temporary, but the effects of how we respond in the midst of the event will last much longer. A poor attitude in the midst of the storm can cause the storm to rage inside for a lifetime."

It's worth repeating that the attitude we choose makes us or breaks us. It reminds me of the story by Michael Hodgin about two Kentucky racing stable owners who had developed a rivalry.

Each spring they both entered a horse in a local steeplechase. One of them thought that having a professional rider might give his horse an edge in the race, so he hired a hotshot jockey.

Well, the day of the race finally came, and as usual, their two horses were leading the race right down to the last fence. But the final fence was too much for both of the horses. Both of them fell, and both riders were thrown. But that didn't stop the professional jockey. He remounted quickly and easily won the race.

When he got back to the stable, he found the horse owner fuming with rage. The jockey really didn't understand the owner's behavior, because he won the race. So the jockey asked, "What's the matter with you? I won the race, didn't I?"

The red-faced owner nodded, "Oh yes, you won the race. But you won it on the wrong horse!"

Sometimes we cause our own disappointments, and at times other people cause them. In order to be successful in leading others, you have to successfully lead yourself. When you get knocked down, you get back up, you choose the attitude that you will lead with, and you set the tone for the attitude that others around you will have also.

Dr. Norman Vincent Peale illustrates this concept in his book *Power of the Plus Factor*: "Once walking through the twisted little streets of Kowloon in Hong Kong, I came upon a tattoo studio. In the window were displayed samples of tattoos available.

"On the chest or arms you could have tattooed an anchor or flag or mermaid or whatever. But what struck me with force were three words that could be tattooed on one's flesh, *Born to Lose*.

"I entered the shop in astonishment and, pointing to those words, asked the Chinese tattoo artist, 'Does anybody really have that terrible phrase *Born to Lose* tattooed on one's body?'

"He replied, 'Yes, sometimes.' 'But,' I said, 'I just can't believe that anyone in his right mind would do that.' The Chinese man simply tapped his forehead and in broken English said, 'Before tattoo on body, tattoo on mind.'"

The collective state of mind or attitude within your organization sets the course for where it's headed. Maintaining a healthy attitude is essential to success.

To position an organization to be a winner, each leader should possess, inventory, and exemplify three basic ingredients.

You must choose correct thoughts. Identify not just the thought processes you have but their consequences. What are your thoughts about work, your coworkers, your company's values and goals? Have you bought in to them, or do you hold them in contempt?

You may be saying to yourself, "You don't know the jerks I work with." I may not know about the particulars of your circumstances, but I do know that the first secret to creating a positive workplace attitude begins in one heart at a time.

Sydney Harris summed it up wisely when he mused, "The underdog who condemns the behavior of the overdog rarely stops to consider whether his attitude would be any different if destiny had consigned him to be the role of the overdog." A positive workplace attitude begins with one person at a time. Let it begin with you.

You must choose productive attitudes. Simply put, everyone has an attitude. The question is, is yours a productive one? A positive attitude is essential. The productivity of your organization depends on the success of the people in it.

Golf legend Arnold Palmer has a plaque on his office wall: "If you think you are beaten, you are. If you think you dare not, you don't. If you'd like to win but think you can't, it's almost certain that you won't. Life's battles don't always go to the stronger or faster man, but sooner or later, the man who wins is the man who thinks he can."

Productivity in your organization is the blessing of those who choose the right attitude. As a result, everyone wins. Ask yourself, "Has my attitude contributed in a substantial way to the success of the organization?" When you choose your attitude wisely, the answer should come easily.

When people lay aside petty differences that prevent progress and join together in unity of attitude and purpose, great things can happen. President Dwight D. Eisenhower's rule for his office staff was as follows: "I want everyone smiling around here. Always take your job seriously, but never yourself. Don't forget to pray."

Workplace attitudes are built one attitude at a time. What does your attitude say about the direction of where your organization is headed?

Organizational attitudes are the sum of the personal attitudes that work in it. But what happens when the organization takes a dive? Even the best of leaders are not exempt from setbacks and potential threats. As a leader, how you respond makes all the difference.

On a wintry day in January 2009, US Airways Flight 1549 taxied down the runway at New York's LaGuardia Airport. The flight bound for Charlotte, North Carolina, was a familiar one for Capt. Chesley "Sully" Sullenberger. Minutes after takeoff, Flight 1549 was floating in the Hudson River; mechanical failure from a bird shot brought the plane down.

In his book, *Highest Duty: My Search for What Really Matters,* Sullenberger shares not only his life story but the heroic actions he and his crew took to ensure that not one passenger was lost.

Sullenberger writes, "Through the media, we have all heard about ordinary people who find themselves in extraordinary situations. They act courageously or responsibly, and their efforts are described as if they opted to act that way on the spur of the moment. We've all read the stories: the man who jumps onto a subway track to save a stranger, the firefighter who enters a burning building knowing the great risks, the teacher who dies protecting his students during a shooting.

"I believe many people in those situations actually have made decision years before. Somewhere along the line, they came to define the sort of person they wanted to be, and then they conducted themselves accordingly. They had told themselves they would not be passive observers. If called upon to respond in some courageous or selfless way, they would do so."

Sullenberger describes what makes leaders tick. The courageous acts that so many people demonstrated that January day result from daily decisions made long before they were placed in that situation.

You must choose to exemplify courage. Not only did the crew of Flight 1549 act with courage, but so did emergency personnel on the scene, including ordinary citizens on the ferryboats who assisted in the rescue.

"Courage is not the absence of fear," said Ambrose Redmoon, "but rather the judgment that something else is more important than fear." Everyday leaders who came to the rescue of the passengers set fear aside and did what had to be done.

Your organization may not be facing a life-or-death emergency like that of Flight 1549, but courageous actions are being called upon for sound leadership, a fresh approach, a new vision. Summon within yourself a courageous attitude and dare to lead.

Everyday leaders assess risk and respond. In the initial moments after the bird strike, Sully and copilot Jeff Sikes had to rely on their extensive training and instincts in order to pull off the impossible.

At the controls of a descending, crippled airplane, Sully had to make split-second decisions that would mean the difference between life and death for all on board.

The distance to nearby airports and the rapid rate of descent of the plane compounded an already difficult situation. Sully had no choice but to put the plane in the Hudson River. While not the optimum choice, it was the right one, and all were saved.

Risk can be frightening in some circumstances. Leaders understand what E. E. Cummings noted: "Once we believe in ourselves, we can risk curiosity, wonder, spontaneous delight, or experience that reveals the human spirit." When channeled properly, risk can get you out of your comfort zone and propel you to the next level. This attitude can give you the momentum you need to move forward and experience a new level of growth for your organization.

Everyday leaders bring out the best in others. Whether it was air traffic controllers, the flight crew, or emergency services personnel, everyday leaders rose to the occasion to bring order out of chaos. The way they acted on the spur of the moment is testimony to the power of the human spirit, in times of adversity, to do the right thing.

As everyday leaders, you are the guardians of servitude and the custodians of courage in these times. You tap the resources of leadership not out of impulse but from what you have nurtured within all along.

Booker T. Washington said, "Character, not circumstances, make the man." That is true in leadership, and that is true by the attitude that you choose. The events and circumstances of that January day did not make Sully Sullenberger a leader or a hero; they just revealed it.

The attitude you choose is the defining characteristic of your leadership. In times of prosperity and success, as well as in times of uncertainty and trial, your attitude makes you or breaks you. Choose your attitude carefully.

CHAPTER SIX

AUTHENTICITY

John Maxwell shares a story about a man who suffered from constant headaches who went to see his doctor.

"I don't know why I keep getting these terrible headaches," he lamented. "I don't drink like so many other people do. I don't smoke like so many other people do. I don't overeat like so many other people do. I don't run around like so many other people do. I don't—"

At that point, the doctor interrupted him. "Tell me," the physician stated. "This pain you complain of, is it a sharp shooting pain?"

"Yes," the man answered.

"And does it hurt here, here, and here?" the doctor asked, indicating places around his head.

"Yes," the man replied hopefully, "that's it exactly."

"Simple," the doctor said, rendering his diagnosis. "Your problem is that you have your halo on too tight."

Leaders come in every style and manner imaginable. While no leader is perfect, certain warning signs—red flags, if you will—must be identified that present challenges to authenticity. The call to authentic leadership begins when we expose the red flags that prevent authentic leadership from flourishing. Three types of leaders are a direct challenge to authentic leadership.

The leader with the halo, like the man in the joke, *has an image issue.* The great philosopher Popeye said, "I am what I am." But for the leader with the halo, his real identity is a mystery. Perception over reality is precisely what he prefers.

Authenticity is a foundation stone of success for any leader, and the road to success—as we've discussed—is paved with setbacks, disappointments, and failures. While humanity is sometimes perceived as a sign of weakness, the leader with the halo can find great fulfillment when coming to terms with his humanity. Not only is it liberating but the leader's humanity usually comes as no surprise to those around him.

The leader with the inflated ego has a realness issue. How many leaders have you encountered who are so stuck on themselves that they are unpleasant to be around? A fundamental difference exists between confidence in one's abilities and gifts to succeed (humility) and artificial self-worth (arrogance).

Authentic leadership has a vested interest in the lives and well-being of others. In the life of your organization and the credibility of your leadership style, is there anything more important? Dale Carnegie said, "You can make more friends in two months by becoming interested in other people than you can in two years by trying to get other people interested in you."

A fundamental difference separates a healthy perception of your God-given talents (a gift) and a self-assumption (pretense) that alienates you.

A wise leader serves in humility with a grateful appreciation for the gifts and abilities he has. He does not allow ego to derail his leadership, and he leads with authenticity.

The politico leader has a relationship issue. The office politics that controls many organizations may be seen as a necessary evil, but nothing destroys organizational morale more than politics.

Larry Hardiman said, "The word 'politics' is derived from the word 'poly' meaning 'many,' and the word 'ticks,' meaning 'blood sucking parasites.'" When leadership places politics over principle, the life of the organization suffers.

Authentic leaders are relationship builders and are aware of the temptations that office politics presents and the damage it can cause. When healthy relationships exist within your organization, the degree of office politics is diminished.

Authentic leadership is restored when halos lose their shine, egos are checked at the door, and office politics is discouraged. We need, as Barbara De Angelis said, "to find the courage to say no to things and people that are not serving us if we want to rediscover ourselves and live our lives with authenticity."

This type of transparency in authentic leadership can produce powerful results. Imagine the possibilities when authentic leadership is unleashed in your life and your organization.

ESPN's Graham Hays offered a picture of what authentic leadership might look like when he wrote a story about a women's softball game in 2008 between two conference opponents: Western Oregon and Central Washington. Western Oregon won the game 4-2. Both schools compete as Division II softball programs in the Great Northwest Athletic Conference. At first glance, this may sound like a routine game. The events that transpired that day were truly amazing and far from routine.

Western Oregon senior Sara Tucholsky had never hit a home run in her career. Tucholsky came to the plate in the top of the second inning of the second game with two runners on base. A part-time starter throughout her four years, she was the unsung player at the plate about to crush the ball over the center-field fence for the first home run in her career.

Filled with emotion as she began rounding the bases, Tucholsky missed first base and reversed direction to tag the base. Then it happened. Her right knee gave out. Lying in agony from a torn ACL, Tucholsky tried to reach the bag.

Confusion about the rules temporarily left the outcome of her hit in doubt. Unable to continue under her own strength, would a substitute runner nullify her home run? Moments before making the decision to bring in a substitution, the unexpected happened.

Central Washington senior Mallory Holtman, the team's home-run leader, asked the officials if they could carry her around the bases. Holtman and shortstop Liz Wallace lifted Tucholsky off the ground and supported her weight between them as they carried her around the bases. They stopped at each base until they carried her across home plate into the waiting arms of her teammates.

As the trio crossed home plate, the crowd stood and cheered their incredible display of sportsmanship. Holtman and Wallace returned to the field and tried to win the game, but that display decidedly was the most memorable part of the day.

Leadership exploits show up in unexpected ways and are demonstrated by unsung heroes. The selfless, authentic acts of leadership exhibited each day give hope as we look at the leaders of tomorrow. Here are three reasons to be optimistic.

Leaders step up at the right time. The young ladies who carried Tucholsky around the bases had every reason not to do it. But they realized at the end of the day what was most important was not winning or losing a ball game, but a demonstration of a random act of kindness.

The right time to step up is not dictated by circumstances, when it is time to close a deal, or when a championship is on the line. Character's high calling to humility can be demonstrated in boardrooms and on ball fields at any given time.

Leaders step up at the right place. The sportsmanship of Holtman and Wallace was remarkable. Everything that the team had worked so hard to achieve was on the line. Without prompting or coercion these ladies placed the team in a position that ultimately cost them the game, but one that set them apart as authentic leaders.

My belief is that the underlying principles of leadership

were already intact with these athletes. A leader understands that her time to step up may come when least expected. Holtman and Wallace were in the right place at the right time and allowed their leadership to shine.

Leaders step up for the right reasons. Leadership is about seizing opportunities when presented. Tucholsky had never hit a home run in her career. Holtman held her school's record for them. They could not have been further apart in terms of their respective abilities. Holtman knew what this home run would mean to her and thus offered to carry her around the bases. In leadership, being right is not as important as doing the right thing.

Western Oregon coach Pam Knox put the game in perspective, saying, "It was such a lesson we all learned—that it is not all about winning. And we forget that, because as coaches, we are always trying to get to the top. We forget that. But I will never, ever forget this moment. It has changed me, and I am sure it has changed my players."

The Central Washington women's softball team teaches us that whether in business, sports, or life, to get ahead and have a greater victory you have to give someone else a lift.

Authentic leaders understand the power and possibilities of their leadership. At one time, it is told, Andrew Carnegie was the wealthiest man in America. He came to America from his native Scotland when he was a small boy. He did a variety of odd jobs and eventually ended up as the largest steel manufacturer in the United States. At one time he had forty-three millionaires working for him. In those days a millionaire was a rare person. Conservatively speaking, a million dollars would be equivalent to at least $20 million today.

A reporter asked Carnegie how he had hired forty-three millionaires. Carnegie responded that those men had not been millionaires when they started working for him but had become millionaires as a result.

The reporter's next question was, "How did you develop these men to become so valuable to you that you have paid them this much money?" Carnegie replied that men are developed the same way gold is mined. When gold is mined, several tons of dirt must be moved to get an ounce of gold, but one doesn't go into the mine looking for dirt—one goes into the mine looking for gold.

Carnegie teaches a valuable lesson for authentic leaders that is all too often forgotten. We tend to look for the flaws in others instead of their potential. While finding flaws and picking them apart might be easier, an authentic leader looks for and finds in others the good qualities and nurtures them.

An authentic leader develops what I refer to as leadership margins. One definition of the word "margins," as it appears in the *American Heritage Dictionary*, is "an amount allowed beyond what is needed: a margin of safety."

We find safety and comfort living within margins. We tote the line and expect others to do the same. Yet as leaders we need to develop margins and expand in order to add value to others. Authentic leaders allow themselves to be stretched and see their leadership margins expanded. Four specific margins that can be expanded significantly increase influence as a leader.

Consider the margin of grace. A leader needs a strong degree of grace when positioning an organization for success. Failure happens. People make mistakes. Setbacks occur on the road to success. A leader needs margins of grace—an amount allowed beyond what is needed.

Jeffrey Zaslow, in *Tell Me All about It*, recalls the story of his father coaching a team of eight-year-olds in baseball. "He had a few excellent players, and some who just couldn't get the hang of the game. Dad's team didn't win once all season. But in the last inning of the last game, his team was only down by a run. There was one boy who had never been able to hit the ball—or catch it. With two outs, it was his turn to bat. He surprised the world and got a single!

"The next batter was the team slugger. Finally, Dad's team might win a game. The slugger connected, and as the boy who hit the single ran to second, he saw the ball coming toward him. Not certain of baseball's rules, he caught it. Final out! Dad's team lost.

"Quickly, my father told his team to cheer. The boy beamed. It never occurred to him that he lost the game. All he knew was he had hit the ball and caught it—both for the first time. His parents later thanked my dad. Their child never even got in a game before that season. We never told the boy exactly what happened. We didn't want to ruin it for him. And 'til this day, I'm proud of what my father did that afternoon."

Margins of grace in your organization speak volumes on your leadership. How generous will you be with it?

Consider the margin of confidence. Confidence is the fuel that powers your organization. Confidence matters because of its residual impact. Instilling confidence is not a short-term fix to get through a segmented time frame. Certainly the benefit of confidence is sustaining during challenging times, but confidence is to be built upon.

One of the qualities of a leader is to inspire confidence among the team. If the team is not clicking on all cylinders, if setbacks prevail more than progress, then margins of confidence need to be expanded.

American painter John Sargent once painted a panel of roses that his critics praised highly. It was a small picture, but it approached perfection. Although offered a high price for it on many occasions, Sargent refused to sell it. He considered it his best work and was very proud of it. Whenever he was deeply discouraged and doubtful as an artist, he would look at it and remind himself, "I painted that." Then his confidence and ability would come back to him.

People in your organization need a leader with expanded margins of confidence to remind them that their best days are ahead of them. Build your team in abundant margins of confidence, and watch them reach new levels previously unattained.

Consider the margin of creativity. A wise leader encourages outside-the-box thinking in order to position his team for success.

In addition to Mount Rushmore, one of Gutzon Borglum's great works as a sculptor is the head of Lincoln in the Capitol in Washington, D.C.; he cut it from a large square block of stone in his studio. One day, when the face of Lincoln was just becoming recognizable out of the stone, a young girl was visiting the studio with her parents. She looked at the emerging face of Lincoln, her eyes registering wonder and astonishment.

She stared at the piece for a moment and then ran to the sculptor. "Is that Abraham Lincoln?" she asked.

"Yes."

"Well," said the little girl, "how in the world did you know he was in there?"

Sometimes it takes a little creativity in the margins to realize a team's potential. A good leader values team members who think differently and challenge old assumptions.

Consider the margin of personal development. An authentic leader is constantly growing, developing, and expanding his knowledge and margins as a leader. A generous margin of personal development is the product of the leader who understands that at the perimeters of the organization are team members who are ready to take the team to new levels.

A reporter once approached Pablo Casals at the age of ninety-five and asked him, "Mr. Casals, you are ninety-five and the greatest cellist who ever lived. Why do you still practice six hours a day?"

Casals answered, "Because I think I am making progress."

Authentic leaders know that personal growth and development are achieved through diligence and commitment. As you commit yourself to expanding these margins in your life, you will see the margins expand in your organization.

Authenticity is one of the highest callings in leadership. Imagine the possibilities of your leadership as you lead not from the position of what you know but from the power and integrity of your heart.

PART THREE

BORDERS THAT DEFINE US—THE MEASURE OF OUR LEADERSHIP

CHAPTER SEVEN

LOYALTY

Businesses depend upon many factors for success. Among them are a solid business plan, sound leadership, and a strong team of individuals committed to its success. One of the key ingredients is loyalty.

I had the privilege some time ago to have dinner with some executives from Chick-fil-A. It was a delightful experience. One of the things that impressed me during our time together was their absolute commitment to the philosophy of Chick-fil-A and the manner in which they spoke so highly of their boss, Truett Cathy. Cathy is legendary, and his success story is truly an inspiration.

In his book *Eat More Chicken: Inspire More People*, Cathy has a chapter titled "The Loyalty Factor." In the chapter he lays out the mechanics of how the company selects its Operators and what is expected of them.

The concept of loyalty he presents is inspiring, and every smart leader would be wise to emulate it. His thesis is nothing new, but wise in its practicality. How loyalty is built, sustained, and implemented in your organization is critical. Consider these approaches as you build loyalty among your team.

Loyalty is built through relationship. Cathy writes, "The more we can foster the feeling that we are a group of people working together, depending on each other, and not just bound by a franchise agreement, the more likely we are to be loyal to each other."

The issue of relationship extends beyond a contract that binds people together. Corporately, Chick-fil-A places a strong emphasis on family. Cathy states, "This is one of the most important principles we live by: The family comes first. We tell Operators that the worst thing that can happen, other than to drop dead, is to lose your family. What does a man gain if he gains the whole world and loses his family?"

Cathy understands what many executives wish they did. Making all the money in the world is a hollow victory if it comes at the expense of losing your family. Loyalty to your family precedes loyalty to your organization.

Loyalty is built through trust. Every successful organization has it. Without trust, it is impossible to succeed. Sadly what we find in many organizations is a demand for loyalty that is expected to flow from the bottom up. In other words, leadership at the top expects loyalty from subordinates that is typically driven by insecurity. It's not built out of respect; neither is the loyalty mutual. It's one-sided. This mentality is archaic and is a prescription for disaster in any organization.

A successful organization is built on mutual respect and trust. Cathy writes, "Success in any relationship or endeavor begins with trust. It's amazing how much you can accomplish when you trust the people around you and they trust you."

Trust evolves from relationships. Cathy explains, "I trust my management team to run the company from the inside. Trusting them doesn't mean I never question a decision. It's good for them to realize the decision can be challenged, and that I want them to be thoughtful in the conclusions and sure of their convictions."

Loyalty is principle driven. Cathy acknowledges that much time and energy are devoted to the selection process of new franchise operators. "Our Operators consider themselves to be mentors to the next generation." That approach in turn helps to narrow the search in the selection process. As Cathy writes,

"We don't hire people because they need a job. We hire people because we need them."

Cathy's insights are useful in daily leadership: loyalty is built through relationships and trust and are driven by core principles. Loyalty is a true measure of your leadership, and your impact is defined by it.

One of the all-time greats in baseball was Babe Ruth. His bat had the power of a cannon, and his record of 714 home runs remained unbroken until Hank Aaron came along. The Babe was the idol of sports fans, but in time age took its toll, and his popularity began to wane.

Finally the Yankees traded him to the Braves. In one of his last games in Cincinnati, Babe Ruth began to falter. He struck out and made several misplays that allowed the Reds to score five runs in one inning. As the Babe walked toward the dugout, chin down and dejected, there rose from the stands an enormous storm of boos and catcalls. Some fans actually shook their fists.

Then a wonderful thing happened. A little boy jumped the railing, and with tears streaming down his cheeks he ran out to the great athlete. Unashamedly the boy flung his arms around the Babe's legs and held on tightly. Babe Ruth scooped him up, hugged him, and set him down again. Patting him gently on the head, the Babe took his hand, and the two of them walked off the field together.

The story of Babe Ruth serves as a great reminder of the power of loyalty as seen through the innocence of a child. Not deterred by the advantage of having years to watch Ruth's game decline, the young boy still esteemed the baseball great for what he was, not for what he had become in his twilight years.

Through the eyes of an unnamed boy come principles of loyalty and compassion that can empower leaders for greater service. The most effective means by which to empower your team and solidify your leadership comes down to these simple lessons.

In success you gather a following. When the Babe was on top of his game, cranking out home runs and winning titles, it was easy to be on the bandwagon. Success is like that. Everyone likes a winner. Irving Berlin said, "The toughest thing about success is that you've got to keep on being a success. Talent is only a starting point in business. You've got to keep working that talent."

While it is normal to understand how loyalty is built in times of success, true loyalty is manifest during the down times. It's just human nature—whether in sports or business or entertainment—to pull for a winner. Loyalty and goodwill are built in the good times, but as Berlin said, you've got to keep working that talent.

In failure you gather your friends. While fans may be fickle, your friends are with you to the end. Babe Ruth achieved a level of success that others in the game would envy. The fans were treated to an era of the game of baseball that was truly inspiring. Yet in the sunset years of his career, he was the object of ridicule.

Somerset Maugham said, "The common idea that success spoils people by making them vain, egotistic, and self-complacent is erroneous; on the contrary, it makes them, for the most part, humble, tolerant, and kind. Failure makes people cruel and bitter." Maugham's observation is spot-on with regard to how Ruth embraced the little boy who emerged from the stands. Instead of brushing him aside, Ruth embraced him, and held his hand as they walked off the field.

Someone once said, "Loyalty is faithfulness, and effort, and enthusiasm. It is common decency plus common sense. Loyalty is making yourself part of an organization—making it part of you." This is the proper understanding of the noble calling to loyalty as a leader. Cling to it during the good times and lean on it during the down times, but never underestimate the power of it.

Loyalty can and should be manifested in various ways. Theodore Roosevelt said, "It is better to be faithful than famous." One such example of faithfulness is found in the example of Dick Hoyt. You might be familiar with the story of Hoyt and his son Rick. I first read the story from ESPN's Rick Reilly.

Together, Rick and Dick Hoyt have competed and finished hundreds of races together. Each time they cross the finish line, they do so at the same time—every time.

Rick is disabled. In each marathon they compete in, Dick is pushing his son in a wheelchair the entire 26.2 miles. Not only has he pushed him 26.2 miles in a wheelchair, but Dick has towed Rick 2.4 miles in a dinghy while swimming, and pedaled him 112 miles in a seat on the handlebars—all in the same day.

Rick was strangled by the umbilical cord during birth, leaving him brain damaged and unable to control his limbs. The doctors told his parents that Rick would be a vegetable the rest of his life, but the Hoyts weren't buying it. Now together, they have competed in more than two hundred triathlons, and four fifteen-hour Ironmans in Hawaii.

The incredible story of Rick and Dick Hoyt is inspirational and one with obvious leadership ramifications. What the Hoyt family has endured and overcome tends to put a new twist on the perceived problems we think we have. By looking at the Hoyts as an example, we find simple truths of the power of a father's loyalty to his son that can inspire all of us.

Experts can be wrong. Peter Ustinov said, "If the world should blow itself up, the last audible voice would be that of an expert saying it can't be done." When the Hoyts were given the news that their son would be a vegetable the rest of his life, they challenged that assumption. Despite being told that nothing was going on in Rick's brain, the reality was quite different.

Just like the Hoyts, you may be the recipient of someone's forecast that, if not challenged, will stifle your entrepreneurial spirit and discourage you from pressing on. The Hoyts didn't buy in to the negative report, and neither should you. I am not suggesting that you throw caution to the wind and not exercise due diligence, but sometimes when your head says no, you have to listen to your heart.

A disability to one person is a marathon for another. Rigged with a computer that allowed him to control a cursor by touching a switch with the side of his head, Rick was finally able to communicate. First words? "Go Bruins!" And after a high school classmate was paralyzed in an accident and the school organized a charity run for him, Rick pecked out, "Dad, I want to do that." Although the initial training was difficult, Dick got in shape and the marathons began.

"Opportunity is missed by most people," Thomas Edison said, "because it is dressed in overalls and looks like work." Dick Hoyt had to train like never before to get ready for the marathons. Dick's devotion to his son was worth the sacrifice in order for Rick's dream to become a reality. When you embrace your challenges as opportunities, then you discover the power of possibilities you never knew existed.

You can go further than you ever imagined when someone has your back. During a race a few years back, Dick had a mild heart attack. "If you had not been in such great shape," a doctor told him, "you probably would have died fifteen years ago." As it turns out, Dick and Rick saved each other's lives.

G. K. Chesterton said, "We are all in the same boat in a stormy sea, and we owe each other a terrible loyalty." Leaders who aspire to loyalty are mutually indebted to one another as together they work toward a shared destiny.

A wise leader understands that loyalty is the life blood of

an organization, the bond of true friendship. Just as Dick Hoyt exemplified loyalty to his son, so, too, will a leader demonstrate that loyalty to his or her team. An unselfish leader models loyalty as a means of asking for it. The reciprocal power of loyalty always trumps demand, and the esteem of leaders is characterized by their humility rather than by their arrogance.

Warren Lamb shares a story of a Japanese seaside village a hundred years ago that experienced an earthquake which startled the villagers one evening. Being so accustomed to earthquakes and not feeling an aftershock, they soon went back to their activities without giving it another thought.

An old farmer was watching from his home on a high point above the village. He looked out at the sea and noticed that the water appeared dark and was acting strangely, moving against the wind and running away from the land. The old man knew what that meant. His one thought was to warn the people in the village below. He called his grandson, "Bring me a torch! Hurry!"

In the fields behind him lay his great crop of rice, piled high in stacks that were ready for market; it was worth a fortune. The old man hurried out to see the stacks with his torch. In a flash the dry stalks were ablaze. Soon the big bell pealed from the temple below: Fire!

Back from the beach, away from the sea, up the steep side of the cliff came the people of the village, running as fast as they could. They were trying to save the crops of their neighbor. "He's mad!" they said when they realized he just stood there watching them come and staring toward the sea.

As they reached the level of the fields the old man shouted at the top of his voice over the roaring flames while pointing toward the sea: "Look!" At the edge of the horizon they saw a long, thin, faint line—a line that grew thicker as they watched.

That line was the sea, rising like a wall, getting higher and coming more and more swiftly as they stared. Then came the shock, heavier than thunder; the great wall of water struck the shore with a fierceness and a force that sent a shudder through the hills and tore the homes below into matchsticks. The water withdrew with a roaring sound. Then it returned and struck again, and again, and again.

One final time it struck and ebbed, then returned to its place and pattern. On the plain no one spoke a word for a long while. Finally, the voice of the old man could be heard, saying softly, gently, "That's why I set fire to the rice."

He now stood among them just as poor as the poorest of them; his wealth was gone—all for the sake of four hundred lives. By that sacrifice he would long be remembered, not by his wealth. He was not saddened by what the sacrifice cost him; he was overjoyed by what was saved.

Leaders understand that loyalty is not about being subservient, but rather putting the interest and the good of the team above their own. From a leadership perspective we learn a lot from the rice farmer's observation.

Leaders pay attention to what is taking place around them. The farmer saw the pending danger and immediately acted. His decision was not predicated on what was best for him in the moment but what was best for the villagers. Loyal leaders understand this concept, and they make their decisions accordingly.

He was personally invested in the well-being of the others. He sacrificed his own fortune to save the lives of his neighbors. Crops can be replanted, the village could be rebuilt, but the lives could not be replaced. Loyal leaders have their priorities in order.

Alan McGinnis said, "We lead best when we seek the welfare of those we lead, when we seek to serve rather than being served." The story of the rice farmer teaches loyal leaders that when we place the interest and well-being of others ahead of our own, remarkable things can happen.

By rushing to save the crop of the farmer, the villagers were unknowingly saving themselves. Unleashing a spirit of loyalty within our organizations creates an atmosphere of devotion to one another that is as powerful as the tsunami—but for good rather than bad.

Margaret Mead said, "Never doubt that a small group of thoughtful, committed citizens can change the world. Indeed it's the only thing that ever has."

Fair or not, leaders are defined by many things: the decisions they make, the successes they have, and the company's bottom line. Yet in the arena of noble characteristics that ultimately define leadership, loyalty is the benchmark to which to aspire.

CHAPTER EIGHT

KINDNESS

In *Perhaps I Am,* Edward W. Bok shares a story of kindness involving Herbert Hoover and Polish concert pianist and later premier Ignace Jan Paderewski. The story is a moving illustration for leaders who are invested in expanding their borders, and it's done through acts of kindness.

Bok writes, "There were two young men working their way through Leland Stanford University. Their funds got desperately low, and the idea came to one of them to engage Paderewski for a piano recital and devote the profits to their board and tuition.

"The great pianist's manager asked for a guarantee of two thousand dollars. The students, undaunted, proceeded to stage the concert. They worked hard, only to find that the concert had raised only sixteen hundred dollars. After the concert, the students sought the great artist and told him of their efforts and results. They gave him the whole sixteen hundred dollars, and accompanied it with a promissory note for four hundred dollars, explaining that they would earn the amount at the earliest possible moment and send the money to him.

"'No,' replied Paderewski, 'that won't do.' Then tearing the note to shreds, he returned the money and said to them: "Now, take out of this sixteen hundred dollars all of your expenses, and keep for each of you 10 percent of the balance for your work, and let me have the rest.'

"The years rolled by—years of fortune and destiny.

Paderewski had become the premier of Poland. The devastating war came, and Paderewski was striving with might and main to feed the starving thousands of his beloved Poland. There was only one man in the world that could help Paderewski and his people. Thousands of tons of food began to come into Poland for distribution by the Polish premier.

"After the starving people were fed, Paderewski journeyed to Paris to thank Herbert Hoover for the relief he sent him. 'That's all right, Mr. Paderewski,' was Hoover's reply. 'Besides, you won't remember it, but you helped me once when I was a student at college and I was in a hole.'"

While many qualities come to mind with regard to leadership characteristics, kindness seems to be one that is overlooked. While some may climb the corporate ladder by ruthless means, kindness is a forgotten commodity that leaders need to rediscover.

As a leader expanding your borders, consider the consequences of kindness as a leadership trait worth practicing.

Kindness given is an investment. The dividends of kindness may not be reciprocated today, but in due time it will. Aesop said, "No act of kindness, no matter how small, is ever wasted." When you demonstrate kindness you are exemplifying the very nature of leadership that is so desperately needed today.

People today are hurting like never before. The challenges many face remind us that we are all in this together. A little kindness can go a long way. Don't be like the man in the *Born Loser* comic strip who asks his boss if he has one good word for him. The boss looks at him and says, "Goodbye." Kindness invested in others is a testament to your leadership; be generous.

Kindness remembered is a reward. Years went by from the time Hoover was a recipient of Paderewski's kindness. Despite how much time passed after that deed, Hoover never forgot. The years that went by significantly changed their circumstances. Hoover was now in a position to return the act of kindness that was once shown to him. This time, Hoover not only repaid Paderewski but the reciprocation was monumental, life saving.

It might be hard to imagine how an act of kindness demonstrated to a stranger today can dramatically alter someone's life tomorrow, but that's the beauty of it. Practicing random acts of kindness is not about being seen or done with an expectation of anything in return; it's simply doing the right thing.

William Wordsworth said, "That best portion of a man's good life, his little, nameless, unremembered acts of kindness and love." Let the signature of your leadership be signed by acts of kindness and lead by example.

The test of a leader expanding his borders comes when his mettle is challenged when he least desires to be kind. Frederick the Great said, "The more I get to know people, the more I love my dog." Dealing with difficult people is always a challenge for even the most seasoned leader.

I am reminded of the story of the newlywed farmer and his wife who were visited by her mother, who immediately demanded an inspection of the place. The farmer genuinely tried to be friendly to his new mother-in-law, hoping that it could be a friendly, non-antagonistic relationship. All to no avail, though, as she kept nagging them at every opportunity, demanding changes, offering unwanted advice, and generally making life unbearable for the farmer and his new bride.

While they were walking through the barn during the forced inspection, the farmer's mule suddenly reared up and kicked the mother-in-law in the head, killing her instantly. It was a shock to all, no matter their feelings toward her demanding ways.

At the funeral service a few days later, the farmer stood near the casket and greeted folks as they walked by. The pastor noticed that whenever a woman would whisper something to the farmer, he would nod his head yes and say something.

Whenever a man walked by and whispered to the farmer, however, he would shake his head no, and mumble a reply.

Very curious as to his bizarre behavior, the pastor later asked the farmer what that was all about. The farmer replied, "The women would say, 'What a terrible tragedy,' and I would nod my head and say, 'Yes, it was.' The men would ask, 'Can I borrow that mule?' and I would shake my head and say, 'Can't, it's all booked up for a year.'"

That humorous story reminds us that, not only will difficult people be with us, but how we respond to them is a universal emotion. Yet the basics of how you treat difficult people sets you apart as a leader. Here are a few suggestions when it comes to dealing with difficult people.

Treat the person the way you want to be treated. It's a timeless principle, but timeless for a reason: it's effective. You may not change the behavior pattern of that difficult person you are dealing with, but when you model courteous, professional behavior, then hopefully somewhere down the line they will get a clue.

Bear in mind that continuously destructive, rude behavior on the part of an associate in your organization must be dealt with in a way that preserves the morale and team spirit within your organization. Never should rude, unprofessional behavior be tolerated or condoned.

An advisor to President Lincoln suggested a certain candidate for Lincoln's cabinet. But Lincoln refused, saying, "I don't like the man's face."

"But sir, he can't be responsible for his face," insisted the advisor.

"Every man over forty is responsible for his face," replied Lincoln, and the subject was dropped. Just as you are responsible for your face, so is that difficult person. It's not your responsibility to change him. Just treat him the way you want to be treated.

Take the high road. Lowering yourself to the level of that difficult person is never the answer. Don't allow yourself to be drawn in to another's bad behavior by behaving badly yourself. Don't be like the man who was told by his physician, "Yes, indeed, you do have rabies."

Upon hearing this, the patient immediately pulled out a pad and pencil and began to write.

Thinking the man was making out his will, the doctor said, "Listen, this doesn't mean you're going to die. There is a cure for rabies."

"Oh, I know that," the man said. "I'm just making out a list of all the people I'm going to bite."

John Maxwell said, "The disposition of a leader is important because it will influence the way the followers think and feel. Great leaders understand that the right attitude will set the right atmosphere, which enables the right responses from others." When difficult people surround you, take the high road, and perhaps others will follow you. But if not, then heed this next piece of advice.

Protect the morale and productivity of your organization. As a leader, it's your duty to protect your team's integrity and morale. Allowing a difficult person to continue in his or her job may ultimately cause more harm than good. As someone once said, "What you tolerate, you promote."

As you act with compassion, act with conviction, and act swiftly, your experiences with difficult people can be an act of kindness that promotes and elevates all involved.

Ultimately, kindness as a leadership trait is an expression of the heart. While anyone can be kind, the truly great leaders are genuinely kind toward others, never forgetting where one has come from or where one is going.

Charles Plumb is a great example of a leader who exemplifies the spirit of a kind leader. His story is amazing. Plumb was a U.S. Naval Academy graduate and jet fighter pilot in Vietnam.

After seventy-five combat missions, his plane was destroyed by a surface-to-air missile.

Plumb ejected and parachuted into enemy hands. He was captured and spent the next six years in a Communist prison. He survived that ordeal and now lectures about lessons learned from that experience.

One day, when he and his wife were sitting in a restaurant, a man at another table came up and said, "You're Plumb! You flew jet fighters in 'Nam and the carrier *Kitty Hawk*. You were shot down!"

"How in the world did you know that?" asked Plumb.

"Oh, I was the one who packed your parachute," the man replied.

Plumb gasped in surprise and gratitude.

The man smiled and said, "Yep, I guessed it worked."

Plumb assured him, "It sure did work. If your chute hadn't worked, I wouldn't be here today."

Plumb couldn't sleep that night, thinking about the man who had packed his parachute. Plumb kept wondering what the man might have looked like in a navy uniform.

"I wondered how many times I might have passed him on the *Kitty Hawk*. I wondered how many times I might have seen him and not even said, 'Good morning, how are you?' or anything else, because you see, I was a fighter pilot and he was a sailor."

Plumb thought of the many hours the sailor had spent at a long wooded table in the bowels of the ship, carefully weaving the shrouds and folding the silks of each chute, holding in his hands the fate of someone he didn't know.

This story serves to remind us of the important little things about leadership and how to expand our borders. When it comes to your organization, what are you packing into the lives of your team? What we pack may make all the difference in the world when it comes to encouraging aspiring leaders to go the distance. Here are some suggestions as to what you can pack to encourage and motivate others.

Pack plenty of praise. Hard-working team members deserve to be praised for what they do. One of the saddest statements to hear at the annual office Christmas party is when the boss stands up to thank her team and starts out by saying something like, "I know I don't say this often enough, but. . . ." My immediate response is, "Why not?"

If your team is working hard and producing results, praise for them should be sincere and frequent. George Adams said, "To praise is an investment in happiness." A happy team is a productive team. Praise for your team should be a priority; it's what kind leaders do.

Pack a good attitude. Charles Swindoll writes, "The longer I live, the more I realize the impact of attitude on life. Attitude to me is more important than facts. It is more important than the past, than education, than money, than circumstances, than failures, than successes, than what other people think or say or do. It is more important than appearance, giftedness or skill. It will make or break a company . . . a church . . . a home. The remarkable thing is we have a choice every day regarding the attitude we will embrace for that day. We cannot change our past. . . . We cannot change the fact that people will act in a certain way."

Never underestimate the power of a positive attitude in your organization. When the chips are down, when the economy is sluggish, when prospects disappoint you, what sets you apart from everyone else is the power of your attitude. Maintain a good attitude at all costs; it is the thread of your chute.

Pack plenty of confidence. As you navigate all of the challenges that you face as a leader, maintaining your confidence will see you through. Keep a steady hand, and resist the temptation to leap when you need to sit.

Richard Evans said, "Don't let life discourage you; everyone who got where he is had to begin where he was." At the end of the day, confidence in yourself, your team, and your mission sets you apart from the others.

And in your reserve chute, *pack plenty of kindness.* Leaders who expand their borders do so with a kind heart. Praise, a good attitude, confidence, and plenty of kindness are timeless leadership traits worthy of attention.

As you invest in the lives of others around you, as you pack their chutes, just remember that what you put in is what comes out. Pack wisely.

CHAPTER NINE

LEGACY

From a story in *Bits and Pieces* comes an inspiring story. Years ago, a Johns Hopkins professor gave a group of students this assignment: Go to the slums. Take 200 boys between the ages of twelve and sixteen, and investigate their background and environment. Then predict their chances for the future.

The students, after consulting social statistics, talking to the boys, and compiling much data, concluded that 90 percent of the boys would spend some time in jail. Twenty-five years later, another group of graduate students were given the job of testing the prediction. They went back to the same area. Some of the boys—by then men—were still there, a few had died, some had moved away, but they got in touch with 180 of the original 200. They found that only 4 of the group had ever been sent to jail.

Why was it that these men, who had lived in the breeding place of crime, had such a surprisingly good record? The researchers were continually told, "Well, there was a teacher. . . ."

They pressed further and found that in 75 percent of the cases it was the same woman. The researchers went to this teacher, now living in a home for retired teachers. How had she exerted this remarkable influence over that group of children? Could she give them any reason why these boys should have remembered her?

"No," she said. "No, I really couldn't." And then, thinking

back over the years, she said amusingly, more to herself than to her questioners: "I loved those boys. . . ."

How blessed that the men had a teacher who loved them and who because of her influence now live productive lives. If you think for a moment, I am sure you can recall a teacher, coach, or mentor who had an impact on your life and helped to guide you to where you are today.

Tim Elmore said, "Mentoring is a relational experience through which one person empowers another by sharing their wisdom and resources." The sharing of resources, much like that of the teacher, is built through relationship with those you lead. Consider the powerful legacy and impact the teacher had upon her students. The same characteristics that defined her legacy are the ones that will define yours. So what did the teacher do?

She accepted her students for who they were. In *Life 101,* Peter McWilliams says, "Acceptance is such an important commodity; some have called it 'the first law of personal growth.'" No doubt her students had already been labeled by others as underachievers or troublemakers, with few seeing any potential in them.

The teacher disregarded the stereotypes about the boys and accepted them not only for who they were but for what she believed they could become.

As a mentor in your organization, act with an expectation that the best is yet to come. Where a person has come from is not nearly as important as where you are leading them. Accepting the people you mentor is the first step in impacting their lives.

She believed in her students. Chosen out of the slums and placed in a statistical category of perceived outcomes, the boys faced insurmountable obstacles. Yet their destiny was changed, not by perceptions, but because a teacher believed in them.

Mark Twain said, "Keep away from people who belittle your ambitions. Small people always do that, but the really great make you feel that you, too, can become great." As a leader expanding the borders of your influence, you must instill hope in the hearts of those you lead.

It's hard to say where the boys would have ended up without a teacher who believed in them, but as John A. Shedd said, "Opportunities are seldom labeled." You leave your legacy as a leader when you have faith in those you lead.

She cared for her students. When approached about the boys she had taught in those early years, she simply recalled that she loved them. It was that simple.

John Maxwell said, "Loving people precedes leading them. People don't care how much you know until they know how much you care." While tempting to measure success by the bottom line, true leaders understand it differently.

Your legacy is measured by the manner in which you accept those you lead, by believing in them, and by demonstrating genuine care for those you lead.

The wonderful thing about your legacy is that you get to write it. You will be remembered as a leader not so much by what you said but in what you did.

One of the highlights of my first trip to England was a tour through the House of Commons. The walk through this historic building was truly amazing. As we stood in the room where the prime minister conducts the famous question-and-answer sessions, the guide pointed out to us the marks on the desk that were put there by Winston Churchill. The indentions, he pointed out, were made during passionate times of debate. Churchill would pound the table with a closed fist, and the marks were put there by the ring he was wearing.

As leaders we, too, leave our mark, our legacy. Like Churchill, you carve out a niche that is characteristic of your leadership.

The type of mark you make as a leader is up to you. For every leader there are marks worth leaving. I feel strongly about two such marks.

Leave a mark of passion. Shakespeare said, "O that my tongue were in the thunder's mouth! Then with passion I would shake the world." A passionate leader shakes the world with conviction and purpose.

In her book *We Shall Not Fail: The Inspiring Leadership of Winston Churchill,* Celia Sandys (Churchill's granddaughter) writes, "Churchill's immense courage in World War II played such a large and varied role in his leadership that we will touch on it only briefly here. But it's clear that when Britain had to stand alone Churchill epitomized Britain's courage and resilience."

Churchill's passion as a leader resonated with his country and eventually propelled it to victory. Passion is an ingredient all leaders must possess if they are to succeed. During moments of passion and persuasion, Churchill left his mark on that desk in the House of Commons. But there was nothing uncommon about it. That passion was a fire in his belly that would never surrender. Your passion as a leader is what defines your legacy as a leader.

Leave your mark with people. The great philosopher Linus, in the comic strip *Peanuts,* said, "I love mankind, it's people I can't stand." While at times we can relate to Linus, succeeding as a leader takes patience, understanding, and skill.

In order to leave your mark with people you have to develop relationships with them. Positional leadership may be the initial starting place for new leaders, but in order to grow to a place of lasting legacy, you can't remain there.

A leader expanding his borders understands that his success is tied to the success of others around him. With that being true, a wise leader cares for those around him.

Leaving your mark with people is about praising them in

the good times and exercising patience in the down times, for-giveness in the hard times, and encouragement in the depress-ing times. Above all else, it is simply about being there.

Like Churchill, we all leave a mark by which our legacy will be defined. Let it be said of us that we were passionate leaders who cared deeply for others.

When relationships are a high priority, building a legacy of leadership is not hard to do—even in the most challenging circumstances.

Consider the humorous story of seventy-six-year-old Bill Baker of London when he wed Edna Harvey. She happened to be his granddaughter's husband's mother. That's where the confusion began, according to Baker's granddaughter, Lynn.

"My mother-in-law is now my step-grandmother. My grandmother is now my step-mother-in-law. My mom is my sister-in-law, and my brother is my nephew. But even crazier is that I'm now married to my uncle and my children are my cousins." From this experience, Lynn should gain insight into the theory of relativity.

That humorous story is a way in which to illustrate some-thing in leadership that is actually not funny at all. In order to be an effective leader and leave a legacy of value, you have to develop people skills and strong personal relationships.

I will never forget the first job I had fresh out of college and newly married. I was working with a wonderful group of young people in a small rural community in southern Mississippi. At the conclusion of a weeklong event that turned out a large number of children and teens, my boss called my wife and me into his office.

At the conclusion of his twenty-minute verbal dissection, where any and everything possible he could think of to criticize was complete, my wife turned to him and said, "We've sat here for twenty minutes and I have listened to you criticize my husband and not one time did I hear you say anything good about what he's done this week." My boss looked at her and said, "I don't call meetings for that."

Needless to say, my tenure with the charming man didn't last long. But the memory of that day has reminded me of the importance of making people your priority and what it means to leave a legacy of which you can be proud.

How you treat people is a clear reflection of the value you place on them. Don't be like the group of friends who went out hunting and paired in twos for the day. That night one of the hunters returned alone, staggering under an eight-point buck.

"Where's Harry?" he was asked.

"Harry had a stroke of some kind. He's a couple of miles back up the trail."

"You left Harry lying there, and carried the deer back?"

"Well," said the hunter, "I figured no one was going to steal Harry."

Sadly, many in leadership make the mistake of treating their team like poor Harry. They fail to remember that they would have no product were it not for the team. If you are going to leave a strong legacy as a leader, people must be your priority.

Relationships are your future. Longevity in your organization is tied to how well you nurture relationships today. How well you value relationships is a barometer as to your legacy. If people in your organization are treated with respect and a conscious effort is made to build a team atmosphere, the possibilities of your organization are limitless. In turn, your legacy is being fashioned for something great.

In his book *Bringing Out the Best in People,* Alan Loy McGinnis writes, "In the simplest terms, the people who like people and who believe that those they lead have the best intentions will get the best from them. On the other hand, the police-type leader, who is constantly on the watch for everyone's worst side, will find that people get defensive and self-protective and that the doors to their inner possibilities quickly close."

The best thing you can do as a leader is to understand that your legacy and the future of your organization are tied to successful relationship building. It begins inside your organization and flows out.

If people are your priority and relationships are your future, then friendship is the pathway. Samuel Johnson said, "If a man does not make new acquaintances as he advances through life, he will soon find himself alone. A man should keep his friendships in constant repair."

Friendship is the recipe that transcends the boundaries of business and stands the test of time. It reminds me of the story of Jackie Robinson, the first black man to play Major League Baseball.

While playing one day in his home stadium in Brooklyn, he committed an error. The fans began to ridicule him. He stood at second base, humiliated, while the fans jeered. Then shortstop Pee Wee Reese came over and stood next to him. He put his arm around Robinson and faced the crowd. The fans grew quiet. Robinson later said that arm around his shoulder saved his career.

A leader expanding his borders understands the value of genuine friendship, the importance of coming alongside a coworker and putting an arm around a shoulder in friendship. A wise leader values, nurtures, and fosters friendships. A leader building a legacy does so while building friendships.

Leaving a legacy and living out the values of that legacy are what leaders are known for. A fine example of that legacy occurred on September 6, 1995, as thousands of fans packed Oriole Park at Camden Yards in Baltimore, Maryland. The Orioles were playing host to the California Angels, and history was about to be made.

The history that night would be voted by fans as the Most

Memorable Moment in baseball history. In the fourth inning Cal Ripken Jr. stepped to the plate and hit a home run. As thrilling as that moment was, history had still not been made. After the Angels' half of the fifth was over, it was official. The fifty-six-year-old record held by Lou Gehrig for the most consecutive games played (2,130) now belonged to "The Iron Man," Cal Ripken Jr.

A Hall of Fame player, Ripken was the ultimate role model for Little Leaguers and aspiring Major League players both then and now. He is a member of the 3,000-hit club, including 431 home runs. Ripken continued the consecutive game streak by an additional 502 games, a record that still stands at 2,632 games.

After breaking Gehrig's record, Ripken said, "Tonight, I stand here, overwhelmed, as my name is linked with the great and courageous Lou Gehrig. I'm truly humbled to have our names spoken in the same breath. Some may think our strongest connection is because we played many consecutive games. Yet I believe in my heart that our true link is a common motivation—a love for the game of baseball, a passion for our team, and a desire to compete on the very highest level."

Leaders who go the distance in leaving a legacy can learn much from Ripken. Are you a leader willing to go the distance and leave a lasting legacy? Leaders who go the distance and leave that legacy understand these three principles.

Leaders who go the distance have clear priorities. Never has there been a time when it is so easy to be distracted by the "tyranny of the urgent." Dwight Eisenhower said, "The older I get, the more wisdom I find in the ancient rule of taking first things first—a process which often reduces the most complex human problem to a manageable proportion."

Leaders who go the distance are individuals who not only have a clear agenda but are executing it. While it might sound monotonous, a fifty-six-year-old record broken by Ripken was done on days when I am sure he didn't feel like playing. Once priorities are settled, it opens new doors to now enjoy the second characteristic.

Leaders who go the distance are passionate. Much has already been said about passion as a leader, but Ripken exemplified what it takes to leave a legacy such as he did, a love for the game. Without a love for the game and passion to energize him, Ripken would not have broken the record.

What about you? What is your passion? The pursuit of your passion is realized when you have a clear set of priorities that guide you and keep you on the right path. Warren G. Bennis said, "The factory of the future will have only two employees, a man and his dog. The man will be there to feed the dog. The dog will be there to keep the man from touching the equipment." It's the same with your passion. Priorities are there to keep you on track.

Leaders who go the distance fulfill their purpose. Leadership's ultimate achievement is not to attain a title or position. It is to expand your sphere of influence for good and to serve causes greater than self. Kenneth Hildebrand summarized it correctly when he said, "Strong lives are motivated by strong purposes."

Now retired from baseball, Cal Ripken Jr. devotes his time and energy to causes through his foundation. He is an ambassador in support of Little League baseball and many other notable charities. As remarkable as his baseball career was, his lasting legacy, that of fulfilling the role destiny had for him, is truly amazing.

In recent months we lost legendary basketball coach John Wooden. Few in the arena of sports and leadership have had such a lasting impact on the lives of so many. At the age of ninety-nine, just four months shy of his one hundredth birthday, he passed away.

Wooden's record at UCLA is that of legend. During his

tenure, the Bruins amassed an amazing eighty-eight-game win streak from 1971 to 1974. His team went undefeated for four seasons and won ten national championships. Simply put, Wooden was in a league of his own and did it with hard work, grace, and dignity that endeared him to players and opponents alike.

One of the standout players from the Wooden era is Bill Walton. Writing in the introduction to Wooden's book, *Wooden: A Lifetime of Observations On and Off the Court,* Walton gives insight into what endeared his players and fans alike to this amazing man. From Walton's insights come leadership lessons that are worthy of emulating and a tutorial for leaving a legacy for others. Here are a few leadership traits Walton reveals about his coach.

Be the best you can be. Walton writes, "John Wooden taught us to focus on one primary objective: be the best you can be in whatever endeavor you undertake." Wooden by his own admission was not the best coach out there. But he was relentless in perfecting the fundamentals that ultimately set his teams apart from the rest.

"The skills he taught us on the court," adds Walton, "teamwork, personal excellence, discipline, dedication, focus, organization, and leadership—are just some tools you need in the real world. Coach showed us how these skills are transferable. He wasn't just teaching us about basketball, he was teaching us about life."

Wooden believed that if he could impart an attitude of excellence to those young men as basketball players, it would transfer to their personal lives in preparation for the real world. What Wooden understood and demanded was not perfection but to simply be the best they could be—nothing less.

Understand the power of right thinking. Walton writes, "You saw how true he was to doing things right, by thinking right. Coach Wooden was more interested in the process than in the result." In short, Wooden believed that right thinking was the surest way to overcome any obstacle—on and off the court. The most important thing was the process and not the result.

Wooden's coaching philosophy was about substance over image; it was about quality, not quantity. Walton continues, "He really wanted things done correctly and it started with the way he did things. You wanted to follow him and his example." What Wooden understood and what he imparted was that getting the result you desire begins not with your physical ability but with your mental awareness. His legacy was that of imparting the power of right thinking.

Be true to yourself. Walton writes, "He taught us the values and characteristics that could make us not only good players but also good people. He taught us to be true to ourselves while also striving to be our best." This is perhaps one of the highest compliments a player can bestow upon his coach and mentor, a mentor whose legacy and impact upon Walton is undeniable.

While phenomenal as a coach, his lasting legacy is the impact he had on the lives of countless people off the court. His faith taught him to value things far more important than a game, stats, and records.

Wooden said, "We who coach have great influence on the lives of all the young men who come under our supervision, and the lives we lead will play an important role in their future. It is essential that we regard this as a sacred trust and set the example that we know is right."

Wooden's success on the basketball court was secondary to his faith, family, and guiding principles that shaped the lives of so many people. As Wooden said, "True happiness comes from the things that cannot be taken away from you. Making the full effort to do the right thing can never be taken away from you." In the arena of sports, Wooden's legacy is forever secure. His legacy as a leader and the contributions he made in touching so many lives are an inspiration to us all, and he will be deeply missed.

Your legacy is the product of your leadership. The influence you have on your family, your children, and your company is only as strong as your commitment to living up to the high calling of leadership.